Self-Discipline

Everyday Habits to Build Willpower and Achieve Success

Luke Thybulle

© Copyright 2023 - All rights reserved.

Luke Thybulle

Table of Contents

Introduction

One day, three best friends, Larry, Ben, and Charlie, decided to go camping in the woods. They were smart, ambitious, and goal-oriented with bright futures ahead. They reached their destination, set up camp, and laughed and talked all evening. Eventually, they went to sleep in their tents.

The next morning, they wanted to explore the area a bit. As they were walking through the thick brush, Larry fell into a hole. It seemed like it came out of nowhere! Charlie called down the hole, asking if Larry was alright. "I'm fine!" he replied. "I think it's a well!" His two friends lowered a branch to help Larry get out.

Suddenly, they noticed a sign that had appeared close to them. It read: *Wishing well ahead! Be careful!* They laughed about it. Soon after, Ben jokingly said, "I wish I had a caramel donut!" To their amazement, a caramel donut appeared out of thin air! Ben and Charlie were ecstatic, but Larry was cautious. His parents taught him to never trust anything that seemed too good to be true.

"In that case, I wish I had a huge bag of money!" said Charlie. Lo, and behold, a big bag of cash appeared. He opened the bag and rolled around in the money with joy. Ben's eyes widened and he made his next wish, "I wish I had a Harley!" Just like that, a Harley motorcycle appeared. "It's just like I imagined it!" Ben exclaimed.

Still, Larry made no wishes. While Ben was still admiring his motorcycle and Charlie rolling around in his money, it all suddenly disappeared. "Where did it go?" Ben asked. Larry looked at his watch. "Well," he said, "you made the wishes 30 minutes ago. So, it seems like whatever you wish for only lasts for 30 minutes." "Then, I wish for another huge bag of money!" Charlie said. But nothing happened. "I wish for a Harley!" Ben said, but still, nothing.

Larry thought for a bit. "Maybe you can't ask for the same thing twice," he proposed. "Alright," said Ben, "I am feeling hungry, so I wish for my favorite junk food!" This time, it appeared. "Great!" said Charlie. "I wish for a luxury bed!" A bed appeared next to the well. Charlie jumped right on it and made himself comfortable. Ben was eating his junk food while Charlie lay on his bed, looking at the trees. But Larry didn't wish for anything.

After 30 minutes had passed, the bed disappeared. Ben, however, said that he still felt satisfied with the food he ate. "I think that when you eat something, you get to keep it," he reasoned.

Eventually, they had to leave. But after that, the three friends frequently visited the well, where Ben and Charlie would make all kinds of wishes. Larry noticed an unnerving thing with his friends—they never talked about their future or goals anymore. They didn't want to work or make any plans for the future. They only wanted to go to the well. One day, Larry said, "This well is not good for you. It is changing you, and not in a good way!"

Larry continued, "You see this well as a magnificent treasure, but all I see is fool's gold. All of the things you hope for here don't last very long, and I think you're starting to become dependent on them. Also, if you don't work for your possessions, you won't value them as much and won't take enough breaks from your constant indulgence."

They didn't want to listen to him. Soon, Larry didn't go with them anymore. In time, his friendship with them ended.

Larry decided to be self-disciplined and work hard toward achieving his goals. He became successful and bought a beautiful house and a nice car. However, he would still live with moderation and control. Many years later, Larry was feeling guilty for leaving his friends behind. He did try to warn them, but they wouldn't listen. He wanted to find out what happened to them. So, he went to the woods.

He barely arrived at the well, when he saw an old, skinny man dressed in rags approach him. "Charlie? Charlie is that you?" he asked in shock. "It's me," Charlie said. "Ben and I decided to come to live in the woods to be near the well. Unfortunately, Ben passed away because of his addictions to junk food and other unhealthy things. But I can't leave the well."

Larry offered Charlie to come and stay with him until he got back on his feet and could be integrated back into society, but Charlie refused. He was only interested in the instant gratification the well had to offer. Larry felt sad for leaving him behind again, but knew that there was no way to change his mind.

In perfect contrast to Larry, they had nothing to show for the years they had spent in the woods because everything they wished for had vanished in 30 minutes. Also, because they never had to work for what the well provided, they never learned important values like perseverance, diligence, thankfulness, and discipline. For many years, the magic well sent both Charlie and Ben into a tragic cycle of self-destruction.

Without self-discipline, nothing meaningful in life is possible. The "magic well" might take many forms in our own lives. It can turn out to be a never-ending search for a "get-rich-quick" trick for certain people. For others, it might be an addiction to partying, video games, or television. Others may never stop pursuing romantic partnerships.

These things all offer temporary satisfaction, but they are all transient and perishable, much like Larry, Ben, and Charlie's story. The only way to achieve true success is to get rid of all "magic wells" in your life and dedicate yourself to practicing self-discipline.

That is the most important thing to do.

Self-discipline is the capacity to move forward, maintain motivation, and act despite any physical or mental discomfort. It is demonstrated when you consciously decide to work toward improving yourself, even in the face of obstacles like diversions, difficulty, or bad circumstances.

Self-discipline is distinct from willpower or self-motivation. Persistence, the capacity to carry out your intentions, and hard work are all factors that go into it, as well as motivation and willpower.

Are you only set on things that bring instant gratification, causing success to be out of reach? Do you struggle with self-discipline, unable to achieve your goals?

If so, come with me on this journey. We'll talk about willpower, what it is and how it works, how you can overcome procrastination, how to set achievable and realistic goals, and how you can manage your time to make the best of every moment.

We'll also discuss resilience and how it can help you overcome obstacles, how you can maintain motivation and focus, and how you can live a life of sustained self-discipline that will only gear you to success.

Most importantly—don't be ashamed. You are not alone in your struggle. I've been there. I have learned many things from personal experience, which means I have empathy for you. I understand what you are going through. That's the reason I *want* to help you. I'll walk this path with you; a path toward victory, self-discipline, and a lifetime of success!

FREE E-Book:
Discover How to Finally Conquer Your Fears

PLUS I'll share with you
My #1 Secret To Guaranteed Success...
See firsthand how I direct my focus to live a life full of energy, passion and confidence.

- Luke Thybulle

www.northstarreaders.com/luke-thybulle/conquer-your-fears

Chapter 1: Self-Discipline—An Overview

We have all been taught discipline as well as the principles of self-discipline since we were young. However, throughout the years, how many people have you met (including children), who scoffed at this and showed rebelliousness and a disregard for those teachings? Probably quite a few, right? But why does this happen?

The Lack of Self-Discipline

What would happen if parents don't teach their children self-discipline, or if it is not taught or expected in school? It can happen. You end up with entitled people, including children, who have little to no value or respect for people, goals, or belongings.

The most difficult part is "controlling yourself." You often know what to do to accomplish a goal (or you at least have the capacity to learn the required knowledge and abilities). Even when you are aware of what needs to be done, it can be challenging to continually work toward your objectives without procrastinating or becoming sidetracked.

Some people steer clear of the subject because they believe it will be mentally and physically taxing. Others decide to stay away from it since it frequently demands us to deal with feelings like anxiety, doubt, or dread. It's also possible that it's challenging to choose what to focus on because of competing priorities. Self-discipline can be harder to maintain because of tough life experiences or difficult circumstances.

Let's look at some reasons that people lack self-discipline:

We're Not Born This Way

We're not born with self-discipline. We need to learn, exercise, and develop it. However, some people don't realize the importance of developing it, or they simply don't know how to.

Lack of Ambition, Willpower, and Motivation

When you lack these three attributes, you lack the foundation of sustainable self-discipline.

Low Self-Esteem

Low self-esteem causes you to feel weak, which also weakens your sense of self-discipline.

Laziness and Insufficient Inner Strength

You'll find it challenging to be self-disciplined when you are lazy and lack inner strength. In this instance, you're likely to avoid actions that require effort and perseverance. People favor comfortable inaction over behaviors that demand effort. Since self-discipline needs effort, being lazy is more comfortable because it is enjoyable and effortless.

Procrastination

People who lack self-discipline tend to put off important tasks. They prefer procrastination over being responsible and prompt.

Giving in to Temptations

Temptations of all kinds come our way, every day. We are exposed to media commercials urging us to purchase certain products. Supermarkets and shopping centers offer a wide variety of goods for purchase, and we are also provided with a variety of methods to pass the time, including television shows, movies, dining establishments, concerts, sporting events, and other forms of entertainment.

How can you refuse to buy the aesthetically pleasing and delicious food in the grocery store or refuse to watch a television program that provides a relaxing diversion from the daily grind? Self-discipline is weakened when all of these pleasures are accepted and pursued mindlessly, without using any common sense.

Negativity

Lack of self-discipline can be caused by negative mental programming and a negative environment.

Having No Goals or Sense of Purpose in Life

If you don't have any life goals or ambitions, you'll likely wander and do little to make your situation better. This can result in a lack of self-discipline.

Fearing Failure

Weakened inner strength results from a lack of initiative and tenacity caused by a fear of failure.

False Assumptions

This is when you erroneously believe that self-discipline is difficult to achieve and necessitates excessive denial.

A Weakened Physical and Mental State

The loss of this crucial skill may be influenced by a fragile condition of health. This signifies that you must take good care of your health and body, eat wholesome foods, and engage in regular physical activity.

Do you relate to any of these? If so, don't be alarmed. First, let's continue finding the roots of self-discipline and what it can do for you.

Defining Self-Discipline

Unlike Larry (who we met in the introduction), Ben and Charlie lacked self-discipline when it came to using the wishing well. Although the well was a fantastic find, he knew that failing to practice self-discipline could change the well into something destructive. Unfortunately, Ben and Charlie abandoned self-discipline and got caught in the trap of wanting an easy life.

Having an "easy life" means you'll stagnate—you won't learn, grow, or develop essential skills. Temptation continually lurks at the door, urging us to abandon self-discipline. We must be vigilant and we must resist! It's only for our own good.

But what is self-discipline exactly?

Self-discipline can take many different forms, including patience, restraint, endurance, decision-making, perseverance, and following through on commitments. It denotes the capacity to carry out your intentions and actions in the face of inconvenience, adversity, or setbacks.

It means having the self-control to refrain from unhealthy excess of anything that might have unfavorable effects. One of its defining traits is the capacity to put off short-term pleasure and instant gratification in favor of longer-term gains or more satisfying outcomes, even when doing so requires hard work and patience. Due to the false perception that it is unpleasant and demands a great deal of effort and sacrifice, the term frequently elicits some discomfort and resistance.

In reality, developing self-discipline can be enjoyable, requires less effort than some people assume, and has significant advantages. It is not, as some may believe, a punishing or restrictive way of life, and has nothing to do with living like a Tibetan monk or having a small mind.

According to Dr. Carjie Scott (2018), it can be divided into three types:

- active discipline

- reactive discipline

- proactive discipline

But, before we dive any deeper into the types of self-discipline, Dr. Scott advises that we make use of a conscious discipline technique—the STAR method. First, practice this method with me. Are you ready? Here we go:

"**S**mile, **t**ake **a** deep breath, and **r**elax."

Did you notice the "star" in there?

Make sure you do this simple-yet-effective exercise first, before we continue. How did using the method make you feel? Remember that feeling—it's essential for what comes next.

Let's discuss the three types of self-discipline.

Active Discipline

This entails immediately taking the necessary action, such as eating a nutritious meal, avoiding distractions while studying, and exercising.

When you are tempted to eat junk food; make the decision to eat healthily instead, understanding the benefits of nutritious meals.

You exert active self-discipline when you set aside time for studying and silence your phone and remove any other distractions.

You choose to be focused on your overall well-being, which means you decide to work out instead of watching television or browsing the internet.

Reactive Discipline

This is managing your thoughts and behaviors when coping with unforeseen circumstances like getting a flat tire on the way to work, handling a rude individual, or locking your car keys inside your car.

You take advantage of such circumstances as learning opportunities rather than complaining. Let's look at some examples:

- You have the tire fixed if it becomes flat. You have the option to choose to be thankful that nobody was wounded and that it was merely a flat tire at that time.

- You willingly turn the other cheek to that rude person. You understand that their rudeness is not a reflection of you. You are aware that "an eye for an eye" leaves everyone blind. You choose to be especially kind to that individual since you know they need it.

- When you lock your keys in the car, tell yourself, "It's okay, mistakes happen.". You understand how crucial it is to forgive yourself and move on. You are aware that during your entire 24-hour day, this is simply one small setback.

Proactive Discipline

This entails taking action in preparation to better manage a situation, such as creating a to-do list, getting to bed on time, and packing an umbrella on rainy days.

Examples for staying prepared for the above include:

- checking the weather in the morning and packing an umbrella if there's a chance of rain.

- making a to-do list in order to prioritize the goals you need to complete by a certain deadline. In this way, you can track your progress and be more productive.

- going to bed at a reasonable hour so you could wake up early the next day rather than stay up late.

Undoubtedly, committing to discipline every day can be challenging. We are constantly faced with problems that seem to arise at the most inconvenient times, so maintaining self-discipline is no simple task.

While it is true that we have no control over potential occurrences, we do have control over how we will respond to them. We also have access to and the chance to put techniques into practice that helps us maintain self-discipline and realize our goals.

The Importance of Self-Discipline

Although gaining self-discipline can be challenging, it is worthwhile because it has the power to significantly alter your life. These are some of the reasons why it's critical to cultivate it.

It Is Within Your Sphere of Influence

You have no control over many aspects of life, including where you were born, who your family is, and whether you are tall or short. However, self-control is one of the few things that you can influence. As such, it is even more crucial to develop.

It Inspires Confidence

You will begin to feel more confident in yourself as you develop self-control. This is due to two factors. First, as you become more disciplined, you'll start moving closer to your goals, which will make you feel accomplished. Second, you'll begin to develop a positive feedback loop that appears as follows:

- Confidence rises when more goals are attained.

- Having more confidence helps you accomplish more goals.

In other words, your confidence and self-belief grow as you achieve your primary goals, which allows achieving subsequent goals to be easier, which in turn fosters confidence. And so, the cycle continues.

It Helps With Breaking Bad Habits

Bad habits are the opposite of good habits. Examples include having a poor sleep routine, spending more time online or on social media than you should, or overindulging in junk food.

Remember that certain habits are highly personal and what is bad for one person may not be bad for another. For instance, I am aware of individuals who are content with playing video games for extended amounts of time each day. All the same, other people would prefer to spend less time playing video games in order to make more time for other activities.

Self-discipline can help you manage any unhealthy habits you may have by either cutting back on the time you spend engaging in them or effectively eliminating them.

It Aids You in Achieving Your Goals

While certain tasks can be completed without self-discipline, the majority of goals depend on it. Why? Nobody will be there to coerce you to carry out your plans at every stage of life for the vast majority of tasks.

As a child, you were told to do things by your parents and teachers who then monitored you and helped you along the way. This meant that you mostly got by without needing a lot of self-discipline. Though, to get things done, you eventually required self-discipline. The beautiful thing about it is that once built, you can apply it to achieve any goal you choose, whether it's advancing in your career, meditating, writing a book, getting into shape, or starting a business.

It Enables You to Carry Out Your Brilliant Ideas

Have you ever had a great idea but never followed through on it? Most people have ideas they later regret not pursuing. You'll be able to turn many of your ideas into reality with self-discipline.

Even though some ideas won't turn out well, this won't take away from the fact that you have tried. And while you're at it, self-discipline will help you give it your best efforts.

For example, self-discipline will enable you to take the necessary steps to launch your enterprise if you have a business idea, or aid you in writing your novel when you've got an idea for one.

In essence, it will enable you to carry out whatever brilliant idea you have, rather than just promising yourself that you would do it "someday."

The Spillover Effect

Progress in one aspect of your life can trigger a succession of exponential breakthroughs in other areas. When it comes to self-discipline, this effect is very potent. You'll often start noticing beneficial improvements in other areas of your life as well as develop self-discipline in some.

My friend used to have no self-control in any area of his life—work, school, exercise. But when it came to exercising, he finally made progress. Not only was that incredible in and of itself, but once he became disciplined, it also became simpler for him to be regulated in other areas of his life.

He soon became more diligent in a lot of other areas, such as his diet, work, and finances, thanks to his exercise regimen. Also, it increased his self-confidence, which improved his social life and self-esteem.

Sometimes, all it takes to start a chain reaction of beneficial life changes is to start practicing self-discipline in one area of your life.

It Involves Developing Healthy Habits

It's important to have things so established into your routine that you routinely carry them out without giving them a second thought. This makes habits truly powerful. Self-discipline is largely about developing wholesome habits that help you adhere to your objectives over the long term.

Your Time-Management Skills Will Improve

Time management is the practice of controlling the amount of time you devote to particular tasks or goals in order to achieve your objectives as effectively as possible. Learning time management and developing self-discipline go hand in hand because time management is a key component of developing self-discipline.

To exercise self-discipline, you must learn how to prioritize your tasks and carry them out as effectively and efficiently as possible.

It Helps You Stop Procrastinating

Self-discipline is essential since it prevents procrastination, which is the act of delaying what you need or want to do. Self-control enables you to start the tasks you've been postponing and reduces the amount of time you spend procrastinating.

It's Advantageous to Your Future Self

We often ignore the effects our behaviors have on our future selves in favor of advancing our present self.

For instance, you may consume a tub of ice cream despite knowing that doing so could be harmful to your health in the long run, only because it tastes good at the time.

You can use delayed gratification thanks to self-control. Therefore, you can reject instant gratification in favor of long-term benefits. The best part of it is that you don't always have to put off your desires. Your current self is equally important.

Yet, self-discipline puts you in control. You can therefore make decisions that are difficult at the time but will benefit your future self.

You Can Use It to Discover Your Sense of Purpose

As you develop self-discipline, you will begin moving closer to your goals. And as you move forward, some of those objectives can lead you on a path you've never dreamed your life would take.

You might discover a profession you wish to pursue, a hobby you adore, or even someone you fall in love with. There is no obligation that you only have a single sense of purpose.

You may discover layers of meaning along the way as new doors are opened through a continuous process of self-improvement and self-discovery.

Now that we know why self-discipline is so important, let's talk about habits you can cultivate to build it.

Everyday Habits to Building Self-Discipline

Bad habits tend to slip away once you begin developing healthier ones. Doing this takes discipline in itself, but as with anything else you do to improve yourself; you'll find self-discipline becoming easier until it feels natural, and you can't imagine living your life any other way.

Whether you're developing new habits or getting rid of old ones—it takes time. Don't rush it—start small, be consistent, and make sure the habits you are developing are wholesome. When you do this, you'll always know what to do next. You'll never be confused about how to practice self-discipline when you are set on cultivating the best habits that can only improve your life.

Let's look at habits you can develop to establish and develop your self-discipline.

Time Management

It can be tempting to say that you just don't have enough hours in the day when taking on a lot of different tasks. Yet, if you can manage your time, you can accomplish far more than you may think. It gives us greater room for reflection and self-improvement, which all serve to advance us toward our ultimate goals.

The key to achieving your objectives is deciding how you want to live your life on a daily basis. Although these activities may not seem significant at the time, they have long-term effects. Our ability to discipline ourselves stems from our ability to manage our time effectively, which is simply a matter of being self-aware.

The number of hours in each of our days is the same. Don't let any of them go to waste.

Invest in Sleep

Quality sleep is one of the most vital investments you can make in your body. Getting enough sleep is essential to getting through your day in a productive way since it is connected to your ability to exercise self-discipline. Your mood, concentration, and judgment are all negatively impacted by not getting enough sleep. Also, it devastates your immune system as a whole and increases your vulnerability to certain illnesses.

No matter what, make sure you get at least six hours of sleep each night. Where possible, stay away from caffeine, alcohol, cigarettes, and prescription medications, at least five hours before bed. Your primary focus should be on maintaining a regular sleep pattern.

Quality sleep has numerous advantages, such as improved memory and decreased rates of pain and inflammation.

Try Meditation

Our minds become more at ease during meditation, providing us with the kind of spiritual stability that fosters genuine growth.

The sounds of regular life fade into the background while one is meditating, which has a big effect on our self-discipline. It's a terrific technique to clear the cobwebs when we're feeling cluttered, confused, or overwhelmed. This helps keep us on course when our day gets off to a bad start.

Controlling your mental health leads to improvement in all areas of your health, from mental to physical to spiritual.

It doesn't take too long to do either! Set 10 to 15 minutes of your day aside. As your mind wanders, keep your attention on maintaining mental stillness until it quiets down. Think of the ground beneath you as the foundation for the energy in your body. Open your palms now and point them upward toward the sky.

The foundation of what we're attempting to do when we meditate is to align the physical body with the spiritual self. You can live a better, more focused life if you can align the two.

And we're not talking about some religion. Our core identities—our values and beliefs, are referred to as our *spirit*. In other words, not only does meditation aid in self-discipline, but it also helps you find balance while improving the well-being of your core identity.

Become Organized

If you're disorganized, it will be quite tough to accomplish your goals. You must thoroughly embody this level of organization in both your work and personal lives. Living a well-organized life and exercising self-discipline go hand in hand. Invest some time and effort if you're not naturally organized.

Start small in your life and make an effort to be consistent. You are free to continue expanding from here, but you are more likely to stick with it in the long run if you start with a specific quantity of work.

Being organized is a habit, to put it simply. And if you maintain organization, you can gradually develop it over time, just like any other habit. It will require work and concentration, but like all the best things in life, the effort will be worthwhile. A calm, stress-free living environment is created by an orderly physical environment. As a result, maintaining self-discipline, even when things don't go as planned, becomes easier.

Try the following:

- make lists

- sort through your drawers

- place items you use in their correct places

Keep in mind that the little things really do matter. For improved outcomes, pay attention to your behaviors.

Evaluate Your Diet

The human body is an amazing machine. In addition to the many things that it does to and for us, it also functions as a massive engine that transforms food into the energy that we need to carry out our daily activities. A significant portion of this energy is used by the body to consume and digest food. In actuality, 10% to 25% of it! (Stark, 2019).

Your body must expend more energy processing the same quantity of food if your diet is high in carbohydrates, fats, and protein. The issue with this, though, is that a significant portion of this energy does us very little good. You should put more emphasis on natural meals, fruits, and vegetables. The biggest, most long-lasting energy boost is provided by these. In a procedure known as the enhanced thermic effect of food, or TEF, they process with less energy while storing energy for later.

Our daily lives are governed in large part by energy. It contributes to our ability to focus, enabling us to pursue objectives and maintain discipline. It is hard to maintain control in the face of poor choices when one is lethargic from overeating. If we can maintain a healthy diet throughout the day, we will have the strength to pursue our objectives and the self-discipline to act on our best judgments.

A nutritious diet alters our neurochemical makeup, which affects both our body and mind. Always choose natural and healthy foods over junk food for a plethora of health-related benefits.

Forgive

It's easy to justify feelings of hate and rage. Sometimes, unfair things indeed happen to us even if we didn't deserve them, and there is nothing we can do to change it. Yet, devoting a significant portion of your day to harboring resentment, shame, regret, or fury only makes matters worse. These are unfavorable feelings that use far more energy than they produce, especially when compared to feelings of love or forgiveness. But once we forgive, we can let go of things in a real way.

Self-discipline is only made possible by forgiveness. When you're not overly concerned with how other people have harmed you, you have greater control over yourself, your decisions, and your life. Your self-discipline is then freed up to accomplish anything with this kind of focus. And the math is actually quite simple: If someone causes you harm, practice forgiving them. You don't have to forget what happened. That's usually just flat-out impossible. However, forgiving and letting go of that toxic energy is possible.

Forgiveness is a step toward self-discipline since letting go of negativity halts the erosion of self-discipline. Although it may initially appear to be soft, insignificant, or unrelated to discipline, it is actually of the utmost importance.

Think about the people you're upset with today and write down your reasons for forgiving them. Consider what you would have done if you had been in their position. Find the humor or try to identify a personal take away from the experience.

Get Your Blood Pumping

Developing self-discipline and healthier personal habits requires enough exercise. One thing does lead to another, so incorporate some consistent fitness routines into your daily schedule and get ready to see results.

Exercise is by far my top suggestion for changing your lifestyle, in case you were wondering. This isn't really a secret belief, as many individuals around the world champion the virtues of regular exercise.

And yet, you still see people who don't prioritize exercise. Now, why do you suppose that is?

We are a pretty busy species. Many of us spend a lot of time rushing around, attempting to get through the day in any way we can. Most people claim they simply don't have the time to develop healthy habits. They are overburdened with work. It just doesn't make sense to exercise.

This is where a lot of us make mistakes. Exercise is a keystone habit that not only helps us develop more discipline but also significantly enhances our quality of life. This action results in the release of dopamine and serotonin, reducing stress and discomfort and improving outcomes.

Our health is directly impacted by exercise, which also serves to strengthen the immune system by promoting blood flow and warding off illnesses. Regular exercise enhances focus, which directly results in self-discipline.

Even so, you don't have to kill yourself by starting out exercising as hard as you can. Begin modestly. Take a morning walk for five minutes, or perhaps another one in the evening. Do that non-stop for a week, then increase it to 10 minutes per day for a week, and so on, until your workout regimen becomes ingrained in your daily routine.

Active Goal-Setting

This is the complete opposite of passive goal-setting in that goals are no longer only thought about, but carried out. You may promise yourself that you would attend to them, but they frequently lack any sort of specific information. Active goals, on the other hand, are documented. They are accurately defined and concrete.

You have something to track when you have a written active goal. They have details, significance, a certain shape, and a quantifiable size. There is a strategy in place to accomplish goals, which aids in both short- and long-term success. When we set long-term goals, we commit to pursuing them vigorously every day. This kind of momentum allows for the realization of one's dreams.

We are all aware that developing self-discipline is essential to reaching our goals. Setting active targets requires direction, which heightens the reality of our goal-chasing. It implies that we are more likely to stay focused on our eventual objective, avoid distractions, and adhere to daily goals.

How do we begin? You must first truly establish a few long-term aims and choose them as a guideline for your future. You'll need engagement objectives for the month, the week, and the day after that. Also, you should develop a strategy for tracking your development week by week so you can see that you are making progress. Tracking and analysis allow you to see how far you've come and make changes going forward.

Your subconscious mind is quite good at making up excuses for why you haven't kept your promises. You'll have the evidence you need to stop lying to yourself and hiding the truth if you use active goal-setting.

Become Grateful

Let's be honest—we're all a little bit like Ben and Charlie. We are constantly craving things. As they did with their wishing well, we wish we had other things, different things, or new things. More of us are distracted by it than we'd like to think. But the straightforward practice of feeling and expressing gratitude can change our focus from wanting to appreciating.

There are numerous effects of gratitude on your life. Whether you're trying to improve your mental, emotional, or spiritual health, being grateful can help you fill in the blanks in your life. It is much easier to lose focus on our disciplines, objectives, and wants when we are living in a state of emptiness and are unable to fill it. When we worry and fret about things we can't control, we become trapped in our own mental cycle. And the ensuing mood of anxiety drives all notions of what we already possess from our minds.

Stress hormones like cortisol and epinephrine are released to help when there is a deficit, which can result in harmful physical problems. Because of this, our immune, digestive, and reproductive systems may all suffer negative effects.

And it's easy to incorporate this positivity into your daily routine. Simply take 10 minutes each day to write down things for which you are grateful. Even if it seems like there is nothing you could possibly include on a list like this, go down deep and find something.

Cultivate Persistence

If you lack persistence, all the discipline in the world won't help much. Without the impulse to keep going after failure, discipline is far more difficult to maintain. This instinct is what helps us get back up after failing.

Goal achievement can be difficult. Everyone would do it all the time if it were simple. It's easy to become dejected when enough time passes and there aren't enough positive outcomes. This is unfortunate because persistence is the key requirement for success. Your life will be built on this type of failure as you go on into ambitious new goals a little wiser and a lot stronger.

In general, sticking with a list of your commitments and being persistent are the keys to success. Every time, a decent, compelling set of reasons for pursuing goals prevails over "truly wanting it."

Now that we've discussed it, we have a better idea of what self-discipline is, what causes a lack of it, and how to cultivate it. Implement the habits provided in this chapter—it will already catapult you in a new direction. But this is only the beginning. How would anyone fair if they lacked willpower? Not good, won't you agree?

Therefore, we'll tackle the topic of willpower in the next chapter; what it is, how it works, and how to develop it.

Chapter 2: Understanding Willpower

Willpower is the capacity to intentionally control one's behavior. People sometimes refer to habits that need significant mental or physical effort as "willpower". Often, these include habits such as quitting smoking, engaging in regular exercise, or setting aside money.

These behavioral adjustments entail withholding immediate gratification in favor of achieving long-term goals, which is a major trait of willpower.

According to Amy Murnan of Medical News Today (2022), despite having different beliefs about how it functions, psychologists generally agree on what willpower is.

How Willpower Works

Murnan (2022) points out two models:

- the strength model

- the process model

Let's look at how they relate to willpower.

The Strength Model

This model was proposed in the 2000s, theorizing that people have a limited amount of willpower that they can use. It is possible to maintain willpower for a while, but ultimately, it will wear down. This is known as "ego depletion" (Baumeister et al., 2007). It is comparable to working out a muscle: An overused muscle will become fatigued.

Once ego depletion takes place, a person has little left in terms of mental capacity for self-control. This is made more difficult by challenges like temptations, diversions, and other pressures. Yet, proponents of the strength model also believe that consistent practice can help willpower become stronger.

The Process Model

Some psychologists started to doubt the idea of ego depletion in the 2010s. In an alternative approach, willpower functions as a negotiating tool between a person's "have to" goals and their "want to" goals, according to a 2014 paper (Inzlicht et al., 2014).

A kid may have a strong desire to play video games, for instance, when they have homework to complete after school. This might be the result of feeling worn out, finding the work tedious, or finding it too challenging. So, they can put their immediate urge to unwind before their long-term objective of earning good grades.

From the outside, this would appear to be a "failure" of willpower; however, supporters of this model claim that it is more about changing priorities. The mind is always attempting to strike a balance between conflicting bodily and mental needs, which might change in priority depending on a person's situation.

This concept proposes strengthening the impulses that result in helpful behaviors and weakening the impulses that undermine them rather than attempting to boost the strength of willpower itself.

What are your thoughts? Is willpower related to either model, neither, or perhaps a bit of both? Either way, willpower affects our lives in numerous ways. Let's look at examples.

Relationships

A study examined how a person's ability to emotionally support a romantic partner is influenced by their willpower as well as their beliefs thereof (Francis, et al., 2019).

According to the authors of the study, those who believed in limited willpower would be more susceptible to mental fatigue than others; making it easier for them to spot signs of fatigue in others. The study's findings imply that this might be the case because strength model proponents were more likely to mention fatigued partners. Some participants did, however, also report feeling more worn out than usual. The overall level of support provided by those who believed in limited willpower was lower.

Health

Changes in diet and behavior are frequently used in medical therapies, especially for chronic diseases. Whether someone can make those adjustments will rely on their level of willpower.

For instance, a study conducted in 2020 discovered that individuals with knee osteoarthritis, who showed unbounded willpower, were more inclined to continue engaging in physical activity as part of their treatment (Maio, et al., 2020).

Yet other elements, like severe symptoms, depressive symptoms, and a greater body mass index, seemed to negate this advantage. This demonstrates how, even when a person believes that their willpower is limitless, their circumstances can make it more difficult for them to exercise self-control or cause their priorities to change.

Academic Progress

According to Duckworth et al (2019), exercising self-control is crucial for academic success. In actuality, higher attainment is predicted by high levels of self-control. Nonetheless, it might be difficult for pupils of all ages.

This is because studying is frequently far less enjoyable than engaging in other activities like sports or socializing. Despite this, many students claim that their long-term objectives depend on their ability to study.

Workplace Resilience

Based on the findings of an analysis by Konze et al (2018), having the mindset that one has infinite willpower as opposed to limited willpower, protects them from experiencing emotional dissonance at work. Emotional dissonance refers to when an employee's feelings conflict with their employer's. Employees may react negatively to news that their boss perceives as favorable, for instance, leading to emotional dissonance.

The authors of the study link emotional dissonance, which is uncomfortable and mentally taxing, to ego depletion.

Employees are better able to handle emotional dissonance when they think willpower is limitless. They have stronger self-control at work and home because this affects their personal lives as well.

Ultimately, this means that your willpower will function according to your belief. I believe that willpower is an example of mind over matter; how much you can use depends on how you interpret it. You may be able to withstand temptations more easily in the future if you believe that your willpower is strong and limitless.

Goal-achieving can be difficult, but that's what makes it so rewarding. Remember, that willpower alone won't get you where you want to go. While you work toward a goal, it's crucial to stay motivated and keep an eye on your behaviors.

Fortunately, you have the ability to manage your powerful intellect. Establish reasonable expectations for yourself and constantly tell yourself that you can and will succeed.

The Connection Between Self-Discipline and Willpower

These two concepts are closely related, yet different. The primary distinction between self-discipline and willpower is that the former refers to your capacity for self-control, mood regulation, and impulse control, while the latter refers to your ability to exercise strong determination to accomplish something tough.

These two characteristics go hand in hand. They assist you in achieving a variety of life goals. Furthermore, successful people tend to have strong willpower and discipline as opposed to impulsive individuals.

First, let's look at both concepts in short.

Self-Discipline

Willpower and discipline are complementary concepts. The capacity to exercise self-restraint, manage your emotions, and suppress impulses is referred to as discipline. Nobody else can take care of it for you: You have to develop discipline within yourself. Contrary to common assumption, discipline is neither about following rules nor being punished for disobeying them. Although you may obtain advice from a variety of sources, the best source of discipline is internal.

Being disciplined gives you control over who you are and what you do. Regardless of your inclinations or impulses, you utilize reason to choose the best course of action. Discipline produces habits, which produce routines, which ultimately result in a way of life. It also provides guidelines for leading an effective and efficient life. If you are a disciplined person, you will be able to make little sacrifices now for a better life afterward. In addition, discipline can be cultivated and reinforced with time, just like willpower.

Willpower

Self-control is a quality of willpower. It can be characterized as a firm resolve that enables one to accomplish a challenging task. It supports a variety of objectives you'd like to achieve. Examples are saving money, getting in shape, or giving up cigarettes. It is a person's capability to suppress an undesired thought, mood, or impulse, or the ability to postpone gratification and reject short-term temptations, to achieve long-term goals. It involves conscious, deliberate self-regulation as well.

It affects many facets of life and is a reliable predictor of life success. People with willpower are more adept at controlling their emotional, behavioral, and attentional impulses in order to accomplish their long-term goals, as they are aware of the benefits of delaying gratification.

Willpower tends to make one happier, healthier, and more prosperous. They are also adept at handling stress, resolving disputes, and conquering challenges. Additionally, they are happier in their relationships than those lacking willpower.

Most individuals believe that with practice and effort, willpower is a skill that can be developed. You can build willpower by setting and completing regular, easy-to-achieve goals (such as waking up at a specific time or turning off the lights whenever you leave a room, getting enough sleep, practicing meditation, and resisting temptation).

Similarities Between Discipline and Willpower

Impulse control is a skill that can be mastered by those who have discipline and willpower as they can delay gratification and withstand momentary temptations. Moreover, these people are more likely to succeed in life. Willpower and discipline are also helpful in achieving long-term objectives. With practice, both can be reinforced and developed.

The Difference Between Discipline and Willpower

Discipline is the capacity to exercise self-control, manage emotions, and suppress urges. Whereas, willpower is the capacity to control oneself or a strong determination that enables you to do something challenging.

- Willpower will help you ignore the piece of chocolate cake on the kitchen table. Discipline will help you follow a healthy diet each day.

  While willpower is consciously and actively controlling behavior, discipline focuses on developing good habits that eventually turn into habitual behavior.

- Willpower will stop you from hitting snooze, help you get out of bed, and go for a run. Discipline will let you get up every morning to get the exercise you need.

  Discipline is deliberate and constant, whereas willpower is an instantaneous and brief burst of focused energy.

- Willpower allows you to switch off the television and do the dishes instead, whereas discipline will let you clean the kitchen first every night before watching your favorite show.

Next, let's see how willpower relates to self-control.

Understanding Willpower and Self-Control

Do we still require self-discipline if we can create positive habits by *hacking our environment*? Let's look into it.

To fully understand the relationship between the two concepts, we have to look at various terms relating to self-discipline, and how they are all working together to help you be successful.

- **Habit:** This is an action that has become automatic or self-controlled over time, either subconsciously or by using self-discipline.

- **Self-control:** The terms "self-control" and "willpower" are frequently used interchangeably, however, self-control only refers to the ability to resist impulses (the "I won't" power), whereas willpower also includes the "I will" power.

- **Self-regulation:** Self-control, self-discipline, self-awareness, willpower, and motivation are just a few of the many internal abilities that fall under the umbrella of self-regulation. It is the intentional, conscious regulation of the self.

- **Self-discipline:** This refers to the persistent use of self-awareness and willpower over time, allowing you to make decisions that are consistent with your long-term objectives.

- **Willpower:** Your capacity to manage your attention, emotions, and behavior in the face of conflicting stimuli and to reconcile your short-term and long-term desires is known as willpower. This involves the ability to suppress your thoughts and sensations, delay gratification, and alter your emotional state.

- **Motivation:** An emotional condition of being inspired to act.

- **Self-awareness:** The capacity to concentrate on oneself and determine whether or not one's behaviors, thoughts, or emotions are consistent with one's internal standards.

The differences are demonstrated by the following example.

A friend Sarah hasn't seen since college comes to meet her. Sarah is astounded by her friend, Tina's, radiance of health and vitality. Tina explains how she maintains a balanced diet and exercise regimen. Sarah is inspired to take her health seriously as a result of this (motivation). She resolves to give up ice cream and start running each day after work.

When Monday evening arrives, Sarah isn't in the mood to run. After work, she is worn out and would like to relax rather than run. She urges herself to run (willpower) since she is mindful of her commitment (self-awareness).

Sarah finishes her run and goes to her freezer to get the ice cream she usually has every night. Instead, she chooses to close her eyes, closes the freezer door (self-control), and has an apple. Once the need to eat ice cream has subsided, she is content with herself (self-regulation).

Every weekday, this process is repeated with little modifications. This is how Sarah develops self-discipline every time she exercises willpower and self-control.

Everything turns automatic after a few months. There is no internal struggle because Sarah runs every day of the week, regardless of how she is feeling. The ice cream appears to be less alluring. She has now developed a new habit.

Your decisions and actions become effective because of your willpower. Your willpower gets stronger each time you resist temptation, overcome a challenge, and reaffirm your dedication to your goal. Willpower and self-control are linked to determination, resilience, and mental toughness in certain ways.

If we consider self-discipline to be the process of weaving everything together, willpower and self-control are the thread. Your first motivation for learning to knit is what led you to do so.

One of the primary purposes of self-discipline, though not the only one, is habit formation. The ability to behave in accordance with your goals requires self-discipline; while some of these behaviors can become habits, not all of them will.

Let's imagine, for instance, that one of your goals is to mend your frayed relationship with your sibling. To establish trust and a connection with them, you must act in specific ways. It is more important to react to the requirements of the moment in a way that furthers your cause (in this case, contacting your sibling and asking for forgiveness) than it is to develop a habit of doing something not related to your goal (like learning how to paint). Building habits cannot be the only solution due to the fluid and unexpected nature of interpersonal interactions; you also need the self-discipline to act following certain moral ideals.

There are no shortcuts to learning and mastering self-discipline. Your self-awareness and willpower need to be strengthened.

Everyday Habits to Building Willpower

Achievement is the result of many little things being done properly on a daily basis.

What appears to be an overnight success typically takes a very long time to develop. Only those who develop the proper habits, and repeatedly practice them, will succeed.

Be Inspired

When did you last experience inspiration? It might have come from a historical record, a great leader's speech, or the advice of a friend or relative. When you are inspired, you can experience an energy rush that can propel you to new heights, which can even make you feel like you've acquired more willpower.

The area of the prefrontal cortex that contains long-term thoughts lights up when you see something motivating. As you start to believe in your aspirations and goals, the neurons start firing and you experience a rush of energy.

In essence, this means that when you are inspired, the prefrontal cortex is strengthened. This improves your willpower and makes achieving your long-term objectives easier.

Question Your Decisions

We tend to think that every decision we make throughout the day is the result of deliberation based on information. However, a large portion of our daily decisions are made automatically. Our brains are operating automatically when deciding what to eat, what to wear, and what to do the moment we arrive at work.

By paying closer attention to the choices that you make every day, you can avoid this inclination. It's as easy as stopping and reflecting on why you decided to get coffee as soon as you entered the office or the reason you choose cereal over eggs for breakfast.

Quality Sleep

The biggest impact on your willpower comes from not getting enough sleep. Your brain cells cannot absorb glucose as effectively when you are fatigued as they can when you are well-rested. This means that you remove the "power" from your willpower.

When your brain realizes it isn't getting enough glucose, it will start to seek sugar and caffeine to make up for the deficiency. Unfortunately, because your brain cells are not as effectively absorbing glucose as they should be, you will not only cave in to consuming junk food but also ingest many more calories than you require.

No matter how many calories you consume, your brain will continue to seek junk food until it has absorbed just about all the glucose from your system.

Fortunately, there are strategies that can improve the quality of your sleep without necessarily adding extra hours.

Take a Nap

According to research (Soong, 2011), the most important factor is the number of continuous hours that you are awake. Therefore, taking a nap during the day can be rather beneficial. It is advisable to get seven hours of sleep, followed by an hour-long nap later in the day, than it is to get eight hours of solid sleep without a break during your day.

The Darker the Better

Almost all of us underestimate the impact that room lighting has on our ability to sleep. Your brain is better able to relax and fall asleep when your room is completely dark. This enables you to get more sleep during the hours you spend in bed, strengthening your willpower.

When You Snooze, You Win!

Your brain will have more energy to use for willpower throughout the week if you sleep more on the weekends. Hence, if you are unable to get enough sleep during the week, try to create a reservoir of energy by catching up on sleep during the weekend.

Use Offensive Tactics

When researchers in the Netherlands stumbled upon a group of individuals who appeared to possess unbreakable willpower, they assumed that they must be saints. They reported less stress than practically everyone around them, ate incredibly healthily, exercised frequently, and rarely procrastinated.

They were not saints, however. Many of them claimed that they would never get up from a bar stool. Some claimed that anytime sweets were there, they were powerless to resist them. These so-called saints appeared to be susceptible to the same temptations as the rest of us.

So, how were they able to sustain such unbelievable willpower?

The answer was that these people just did not place themselves in those circumstances. Their daily routines were well-planned to avoid having to meet temptation. They played offense. They made plans to stay away from temptations that might arise in the future, such as alcohol, sweets, or work-related diversions. They seldom ever had to employ their willpower, which gave them the appearance of having willpower as their superpower (Robertson, 2015).

Find the situations in your life that put your willpower to the test. How can you play offense while removing temptation in your future?

One Task Equals More Focus

Are you ready for a challenge? See if you can list every president of the United States in order of their terms in office. If it's too hard for you, how many presidents can you name?

After you have listed five names, try to continue writing them while also determining the solution to 19 x 43. Don't stop with one to work on the other. Work on both at once, in other words, try to divide your focus.

Did you succeed in doing it?

You have two unique brain regions that contribute to problem-solving. One is your limbic system, which is responsible for your quick and unconscious decisions. Using the bathroom and halting at a stop sign are examples of this. This area of the brain is also short-term oriented, which is what drives you to indulge in doughnuts and switch on the television rather than go to the gym.

The prefrontal cortex is the other, and deals with more challenging issues like how to effectively communicate or more challenging mathematical equations like the one above. Also, this region of the brain is in charge of our willpower and long-term thinking.

Both of the aforementioned challenges require the prefrontal cortex to be solved. You would have had no trouble writing down the presidents' names and solving a straightforward math problem like 10 x 5. Such an equation is simple. You could successfully multitask since you would solely use your limbic system to solve the problem.

Your limbic system is trained as you develop multitasking. Hence, by attempting to do several things at once, you unintentionally strengthen the area of your brain that wants to indulge.

Albeit, the prefrontal cortex of the brain is not capable of multitasking. It deals with too many complex issues. Hence, by concentrating on one task at a time, you are strengthening the area of the brain that uses willpower!

Thus, fight the urge to multitask and maintain focus. This will strengthen your willpower and assist you in making difficult choices.

Aim for a Low-Glycemic Diet

A substance known as glucose is created by the human body when food is consumed and circulates in the blood. The brain requires this as its food supply in order to think, create, and exercise willpower. Therefore, you need to make sure your brain has enough glucose as an energy source to ensure a healthy supply of willpower.

Every food that includes calories will provide glucose for your brain to use. Nevertheless, not all glucose is made the same. Sugary foods will provide you with a short-term boost in glucose levels that will help you maintain your willpower, but they will also induce a subsequent drop that will quickly sap it.

Maintaining a constant blood glucose level is the best thing you can do. This will provide your brain with a steady supply of energy to use willpower over the long run. You can achieve this by following a low-glycemic diet.

Here are some low-glycemic foods that can help you maintain your willpower over the long term:

Go Nuts

Eat more nuts like walnuts, pecans, and cashews that are high in omega-3 fatty acids. Keep in mind that this excludes legumes like peanuts.

Eat Your Veggies—They *Are* Good for You!

All vegetables will contribute to your long-term willpower development, but certain root-based vegetables contain a lot of willpower fuel. These include carrots, potatoes, and sweet potatoes, all of which are excellent sources to boost willpower.

Lean Proteins

Simple, lean cuts of meat, chicken, pork, and fish are all you need—nothing fancy!

Fresh Is Best

Because dried fruits contain a lot of sugar, fresh fruit is preferable. In the short term, dried fruit will cause a glucose surge, followed by a crash. Bananas, blueberries, apples, and cherries are a few healthy options.

If you are not used to eating these kinds of foods, do not attempt to fully change your diet all at once. Instead, concentrate on having them for only one meal each day while slowly and steadily introducing these healthier options into your diet. The best way to eat them would be for breakfast.

Visualize Your Ideal Self

Whenever we stare in the mirror, strange things take place in our brains. There is no activity in the portion of the brain that would normally indicate, "Hey, it's me in the mirror." Instead, activity is in the brain region that says "I wish I were taller, skinnier, or more muscular." In other words, we perceive who we wish to be rather than who we are. We all have an ideal self that we strive to achieve, so this does not happen because we are shallow. We start thinking and acting more like our ideal selves once we have this image in our heads.

Self-monitoring is the best method for sustaining your ideal self in mind. This entails maintaining as much personal data on hand as you can. You can examine the current information about yourself and contrast it with what you really want, just like you would with a mirror. As a result, your willpower will grow and you'll be able to make wiser choices.

The Wonders of Exercise

Exercise is known to be beneficial to our health, but can it also strengthen our willpower? In a two-month study to discover the relationship between exercise and willpower, 24 non-exercisers between the ages of 18 and 50 were recruited to be part of the sample group (Oaten & Cheng, 2006). For the first month, they were only required to exercise once per week, and for the second month, they were required to exercise three times per week.

The participants were put to the test on a variety of self-control exercises throughout the course of the study, from restraining temptations to persevering through difficult tasks.

The outcomes were extraordinary, to put it mildly.

Each participant had improved in their capacity to withstand temptation and persevere on assignments after just two months of exercise.

The benefits didn't stop there. The subjects, who received no instruction from the researchers, also:

- tended to arrive more on time for appointments.

- watched less television.

- saved money more easily.

- showed less procrastination.

- spent less on impulsive purchases.

- started following a healthy diet.

- reduced consumption of alcohol, coffee, and tobacco.

- implemented additional study time.

- consumed fewer fast foods.

- felt they had more control over their emotions.

All of these behaviors came naturally as a result of the regular exercise!

Let's pause now before you make a strategy to transition from not exercising at all to exercising every day. It's crucial to keep in mind that these individuals only visited the gym once a week for the duration of an entire month. That means they only went four times total in the first month!

It is obvious that you don't have to be overly ambitious with your exercise regimen. Establish a consistent, manageable plan in order to start enjoying all of the advantages mentioned above. It doesn't matter if you can only exercise once a week or four times. You only need to create a plan that you won't abandon in order to reap the rewards.

Meditate

Meditation is the quickest and most efficient technique to strengthen your willpower. With this, you can teach your brain to concentrate and resist wandering thoughts. According to research, practicing meditation for 10 minutes each day for just two to three days, will improve your brain's ability to focus, give you more energy, and reduce stress (Oman et al., 2010).

There are many misconceptions about meditation, such as the requirement to chant, burn incense, or dress in robes. So, let's start by outlining the actual definition of meditation.

Meditation is the practice of bringing your attention to the present moment. You will experience the advantages of meditation when your mind is clear and wholly focused on your current task.

Chunking

Chunking is the method of breaking down things such as a big task, goal, or dream into smaller, more doable "chunks."

Anybody who has ever set a goal knows how thrilling it can be at first. When the goal is attained, you can see the "after photo" of your life—one that you probably enjoy. You envision all of the wonderful qualities of the new self and are eager to begin making progress in that direction.

Then, it's time to start working and you suddenly feel overwhelmed, whether you're working with a pen and paper or your feet on a treadmill. You can now clearly see the amount of effort required to move from where you are to where you want to be. So, you become helpless because you have no idea where to start. As a result, you give up attempting or lose the willpower to keep going.

Chunking is effective because it divides your focus into smaller objectives that are simpler for your mind to process.

It can feel overwhelming when you're exhausted on the fourth day of your 12-week workout program.

However, you are much less likely to feel overwhelmed if you change your attention to simply completing the training plan for today. Then, before you know it, 20, 40, or 60 days have passed, and you have never been more certain that you can make it to the very end.

Success is a habit. It consists of numerous little things done correctly each day. Developing even one of the aforementioned habits will gradually increase your willpower. But you have to be consistent.

You will benefit much more if you start one of these daily willpower routines and stick with it than if you perform all 10 in a brief time. Thus, pick one habit to add to your life and make it a priority. Go on to the following one once it has completely become ingrained in your mind.

And when is the best time to start? That's right—today! In the next chapter, we'll cover procrastination and discuss strategies and habits you can utilize to overcome it.

Luke Thybulle

Chapter 3: Overcoming Procrastination

We have all struggled with procrastination at some point or another. Humans have struggled with postponing, evading, and procrastinating important matters for as long as we have existed.

When we temporarily manage to quit procrastinating during our more productive periods, we feel content and successful. In this chapter, we'll discuss how to turn those infrequently occurring productive bursts into regular practice. We'll examine the science behind why we put off taking action, provide tried-and-true frameworks for doing better, and go over practical tactics for achieving success.

Understanding the Nature of Procrastination

People have "put off doing things" for a long time. In fact, the issue is so perennial that ancient Greek philosophers like Socrates and Aristotle coined the term "akrasia" to describe this kind of conduct.

Akrasia is the state of behaving against your better judgment. It occurs when you act in a certain way, even when you know you ought to act differently. *Akrasia* is loosely interpreted as procrastination or a lack of self-control.

Here is a present-day explanation: The act of delaying or postponing a task or group of tasks is known as procrastination. It is the force that prevents you from completing the tasks you set out to perform, whether you call it procrastination, *akrasia*, or something else.

Definitions are great, but why *do* we put things off? What is happening in the brain that makes us avoid things we know we ought to be doing? We should now introduce some science to our discussion. Research in behavioral psychology has identified a phenomenon known as "time inconsistency," which contributes to the understanding of why procrastination tends to draw us in, despite our best efforts. It is the propensity of the human brain to value immediate rewards more highly than future ones (Clear, 2015).

Imagine that you have two selves: your present self and your future self. This will help you to grasp this better. Setting objectives for yourself, such as shedding pounds, penning a book, or learning a new language, truly constitutes preparations for your future self. You are imagining what you want the future of your life to look like. It is quite simple for your brain to perceive the worth of making choices that will have long-term advantages when you think in this manner. The future self prioritizes rewards over the long run.

The present self is the only one that can actually take action, given that the future self can only make goals. You are no longer choosing for your future self when the time comes to make a decision. When you're making a decision, your mind is currently thinking about your present self and aims to attain short-term rewards above long-term gains since you are in the present. The present self genuinely prefers short-term rewards above long-term gains.

As a result, the two "selves" frequently clash. The present self wants pizza, while the future self wants to be trim and fit. Yes, everyone is aware that eating well now will prevent getting overweight in 10 years. However, effects like diabetes or heart failure won't be felt for several years. Does this kind of reasoning sound familiar?

Similarly, many young people understand how important it is to start saving for retirement in their 20s, but the benefits won't be felt for many years. The present self finds it far simpler to recognize the value in purchasing a new pair of shoes than it does in setting aside $100 for the future self.

This is one of the reasons you could feel inspired to change your life before bed, but find yourself reverting to old habits when you wake up. When it comes to the future (tomorrow), your brain appreciates long-term benefits, but when it comes to the present (today), it prefers instant gratification.

Making it as easy as possible for the present self to start something and having faith that drive and momentum will follow once we start are both necessary if we wish to avoid procrastinating—Motivation frequently arrives after starting, not beforehand.

The present self cannot be motivated by future consequences and rewards. Instead, you need to figure out how to bring rewards and penalties from the future into the present. You need to transform the potential consequences into actual ones. This is precisely what takes place when you decide to stop procrastinating and start doing.

Let's imagine, for instance, that you need to create a report. You've been putting it off every day for weeks, despite knowing about it. You feel a tiny bit of nagging pain and worry as you consider the paper you have to write, but not enough to take any action.

Then, all of a sudden, the future consequences become present consequences the day before the deadline, and you create that report hours before it is due. Once the discomfort of delaying came to the forefront, you decided to take action. The consequence had become real, current, and relevant.

Procrastinating often creates more discomfort than doing the work that's being set aside.

Strategies for Overcoming Procrastination

There are several strategies to combat procrastination, such as creating short-term team and departmental goals or clarifying a distinction between your personal work and larger corporate goals. To begin, try the following strategies.

Make Use of Deadlines

It's easy to put off the job when there is no clear understanding of when it is due. You can easily determine the precise due date for a task when there are clear deadlines. Then, you can create appropriate plans to ensure that it is completed on time. After all, if you don't know when the task is due in the first place, you can't complete it properly.

Ensure that there is a deadline for each task on your to-do list. You can use this opportunity to find work that isn't a top priority for you. If you encounter such a task, put it off until a time when you're more accessible or assign it to someone else.

Don't do this just once. At the end of the day, quickly assess the work and assign due dates for any new tasks. In this manner, you will be better prepared to complete tasks when you arrive at work the following day.

Breaking Large Projects Into Smaller Tasks

This is a strategy you'll come across several times in this book. However, it is relevant to each topic and has several uses and benefits.

It can be challenging to visualize exactly how and when a major project will be completed. It's therefore tempting to simply put it off. It can be difficult to understand all of the moving pieces of the endeavor and relate them to your bigger objectives due to its scope. It will be simpler to track and organize your work if you divide the activity (or project) into smaller portions rather than becoming overwhelmed by its size.

Additionally, doing this is beneficial since you presumably aren't in charge of every element of a major task. As an illustration, you would be in charge of planning, creating, and writing if you're doing an article for a newspaper. However, there is usually another person creating the layout, in as much as the piece must also be approved by an editor. The initiative "Write a newspaper article" can be divided into several tasks, which not only makes it simpler to get started but also makes it clear what has to be done and when.

Prioritize

Deadlines sometimes change. This could occur as a result of the team leader prioritizing another project or rearranging resources in response to urgent demands. However, you are better equipped to actively manage your priorities if you are aware of the most crucial tasks. When deadlines and timeframes do change, you will then be able to deliver the work that produces significant outcomes with clarity.

Setting priorities is a smart way to stop procrastinating since it makes it clear which tasks are most essential. You can be sure you aren't working on irrelevant tasks when your priorities are clear. You understand why your work matters instead of feeling like you are wasting time at work.

Use To-Do Lists

Even if you are not working on complicated projects, it is still beneficial to write out each task. Without a simple way to see all you have to do, it's easy to become overwhelmed and lose sight of everything.

By keeping track of every task, you can swiftly organize, prioritize, and complete the work that has to be done. If at all possible, use a to-do list program to log your work rather than a written checklist. While it's satisfying to check items off a list, organizing your work in an app will help you prioritize tasks, add more context, and share them with your colleagues.

Fight Perfectionism

People who continually procrastinate may sometimes be perfectionists. The pressure to produce flawless work is too great in such a situation, which encourages procrastination. However, perfectionism can be overcome with clarity, much like the majority of other forms of procrastination at work.

It is beneficial to have a clear understanding of the impact of your work if you battle with perfectionism. Instead of aiming for perfection, concentrate on finishing the task at hand in the best way possible to support business goals.

Suppose that you are creating an instructional animation for the homepage of your website. This work will be seen by many people, which is making the perfectionist in you anxious. That's because you're concentrating on the result and considering everyone who will watch the video. Consider the purposes and effects of the video instead. The purpose of the animation is to explain the advantages of your company's product to those who are unfamiliar with it: the impact is education.

You can relieve perfectionism's strain and start working right away by rearranging your priorities so that they are based on the impact. Remember—sometimes work that is done is better than work that is perfect, especially if you or your company are on tight deadlines.

Linking Work to Goals

Understanding how your job fits into team and organizational goals is the best approach to quit procrastinating. When you are this clear-headed, work takes on a significant purpose. You are advancing a greater cause rather than working merely for the sake of working.

Ideally, you should be passionate about this vision. Even if you are not, however, just being aware of how your work is related to something bigger can make it feel more important. The work you would ordinarily put off now clearly has worth, which means you may rather be inspired to work than have to struggle with scheduling disparities.

Time Management

Once you have clarity, motivation is more likely to come to you. However, there are still some days when you require a little extra assistance to remain focused. If so, try a time-management technique to reduce multitasking and enter a state of flow. We will cover time management in-depth in Chapter 5.

Staying Focused and Productive

While it is simple to define productivity as completing a task as quickly as possible with the greatest amount of efficiency that is feasible, it is considerably more difficult to truly be productive at work. That is simply due to the difficulty of maintaining focus on a task when there are so many outside factors attempting to distract you from working and being productive.

If you want to be more productive at work, it's essential to maintain your focus. However, it is easy to lose concentration because it is nearly impossible to block out external stimuli in a variety of distractions. How often have you begun something and then got sidetracked when something else came up? It prevents you from producing results.

To accomplish your goals and objectives, you must discover workarounds and deliberately focus. The more you are distracted, the less productive you will be and the fewer goals you will be able to accomplish in a particular time frame.

Your ability to work effectively and meet your personal and professional goals depends on your ability to maintain focus. In the long run, it makes it possible for you to continuously produce the greatest outcomes and supports your success in both your job and personal life. With more focus, you can:

Get Your Groove On

You become more adept at the task at hand and can complete it more quickly and efficiently. You can become consistent and settle into a routine so that working becomes second nature.

Keep Your Cool

You feel more at ease knowing that you can finish the task at hand and deliver it according to schedule. This provides you even more self-assurance to excel at work and effortlessly manage your timetable and to-do list. It increases your motivation and enables you to accomplish your objectives one at a time.

Increasing Output

Your attention span will improve when you focus on your work and avoid outside distractions. You can stay focused on the task longer and continuously move forward if you pay complete attention. You can work more quickly and finish more work in less time.

Ensure Greater Productivity

There is less room for errors when your concentration is improved. As an outcome, you acquire the ability to produce high-quality work.

Everyday Habits to Overcoming Procrastination

It is true that delaying things steals your time. "I'll do it later" results in hours and days' worth of unfinished tasks and assignments. When your productivity or grades plummet and you start to worry about your future, it subsequently develops into something more serious and detrimental. However, if you can find a way to stop putting off your work, all of this can be avoided.

Let's look at some habits you can develop to help avoid procrastination.

Determine the Cause of Your Procrastination

It may have been a while since you graduated from college, and everything around you is stifling the former zeal for work. Partying is more enjoyable than working or doing household chores. Or social media is becoming much more engaging, particularly now that you've found a handle or website that consistently posts a ton of your favorite videos. These are just a handful of the potential obstacles to your productivity. These are some typical causes of procrastination:

- the work appears to be overwhelming

- you have lost interest in your field of employment or study

- the labor is simply too demanding

- you believe you have yet to find the "ideal" time to begin

- you're attempting to rebel by refusing to complete your responsibilities or assignments

You can concentrate on motivation to persevere once you've determined why it's taking you so long to start working. Consider all of the reasons you procrastinate and then do a U-turn. These other habits can assist you in doing so.

Understanding Is More Effective Than Memorizing

School takes longer because you need to comprehend relationships and connections between distinct things. Memorizing can come quickly, as does the evaporation of anything you try so hard to remember. Understanding a topic improves your chances of applying its principles to a given collection of facts or deriving a conclusion from them.

The greatest thing that memorizing can do is assist you to retain a small amount of knowledge in a short period. Everything falls apart when you can't remember how to complete a task. However, when you understand what to do, productivity is boosted and there's little need for procrastinating.

Attitude Determines How Well You Do It

Waiting pays off, as they say. But it's also true that those who desire wonderful things will pursue them. You need to be very clear about why you want to do this in the first place if you want to stop procrastinating and start working. List the reasons you want to succeed in your career.

Today is not just a place you go by; it also influences who you will be in the future.

Procrastination leads to an uncertain future whereas hard work leads to a better one. Decide why you need to work hard and become productive, then act accordingly. The list can be pinned to the top of your desk and used to adjust your attitude whenever you feel like putting off something.

Reward Yourself

Rewarding yourself can be a powerful motivator to do more tasks and stop putting things off. So, feel free to treat yourself after finishing a task. These incentives may include anything from a few minutes of smartphone gaming to a quick stroll or a few minutes of your favorite hobby.

These rewards may also serve as brief rest periods after achieving specific objectives. Even when the temptation seems too great to resist, make sure these activities are controlled in order to refrain from overdoing them.

Organizing

The difficulty of the task or subject is one of the causes of procrastination; however, this can be overcome by remaining organized. Here, organizing might mean a variety of things, such as how you take notes, how you acquire knowledge in class, how you memorize it, or how you go about achieving your objectives.

Once you learn how to approach challenging subjects or projects, you'll be inspired to continue working, rather than just standing there. Make lists and mind maps to help you remember important details as you work.

Your Daily Routine

Humans are habitual beings. It's easy to fall prey to poor habits. You may, however, change your ways and establish productive work habits that will safeguard your future. Habits tend to stick. It becomes challenging to relax when you've established a productive routine since you know you should be working.

The first few days will undoubtedly be difficult, but everything will stick thereafter. Make a work timetable, then go from there. To make sure you are at ease with the times, you might occasionally adjust the timetable (particularly in the first few days). Anyone may benefit from a little hard effort, especially if it pays off in the long term.

Only Bite What You Can Chew

People trying to do a full assignment (albeit one that is overwhelming) all at once is one of the main reasons why procrastination occurs. They do this for a variety of reasons, including to resume having fun or experience that "last-minute rush".

If your workload feels too much, try dividing it up into manageable portions. After that, you can give those portions of time. For each chunk, a day or a few hours should be allotted, depending on how complex the task is. That means you are forced to concentrate on just one tiny portion at a time. Students have the option of reading a few pages from their textbook, answering five to six multiple-choice questions, or finding some references for their papers.

Now that we understand the dangers of procrastination and how to overcome it, we need something to work toward, right? Therefore, the next chapter will deal with goals—how to set them, which type of goals to set, and habits that can help achieve them.

Chapter 4: Setting and Achieving Goals

What made Larry different from Ben and Charlie? Yes, he had a vision, he was disciplined and dedicated to achieving his goals, his success didn't come easy, and nothing he gained was simply wished for. Nonetheless, hard work and perseverance paid off and allowed him to live comfortably. What is your life like? Do you pursue goals, or do they remain fleeting dreams in your mind? Have you set up camp near a "wishing well", hoping that life will reward you without the effort of showing resolve?

Having dreams is good, but they will not satisfy you. Wishing for things won't bring you comfort. Larry successfully pursued his goals, but that's the catch—he had to *set* goals before they could be pursued.

In this chapter, we'll talk about goal-setting and how to ensure that they are realistic and achievable. It's time to turn your dreams into reality!

Understanding the Importance of Goal-Setting

The whole world is a little dispersed. Numerous organizations put a lot of effort into trying to bring order to the everyday chaos; yet, everything from our relationships to the definition of success remain, at best, vague. However, the dynamic network that links us all can be a source of meaning, purpose, and success for those prepared to invest the time and conduct some introspection. Let's examine the factors that make goal-setting so essential for success.

Goals Encourage Movement

For example, let's imagine a baseball player. Baseball is an intricate sport with a wide range of metrics that all highlight the importance of a player's participation in both general and specific circumstances. Let's imagine that our baseball player is a frequent home run hitter, but his team keeps losing. By all accounts, our player is performing admirably and scoring goals.

But after a little investigation, it becomes clear that he only hits well when the game is ahead. This player now has a target and a purpose after previously lacking any meaningful desire to alter or enhance his skills. He can keep moving forward even when the hours are long and he feels physically exhausted by identifying this area for improvement and setting an achievable target.

In the same way, we must find a reason or motivation to push us forward, even when things don't seem to go our way. This is what makes setting a goal essential.

Goals Boost Morale

Your metrics and goals are fantastic, but people are what make success a reality. Because of this, concern for people needs to be your primary focus. In doing so, you can prevent the burnout of important team members and maintain your leadership when times are difficult. As much as we'd like to, we are not calculators who process facts without feeling joy or sorrow. Give everyone something to strive for, fight for, and win for in order to keep your team, your organization, and yourself content.

Goals Express Relevance

Setting targets not only clarifies priorities and success as an outcome but also conveys that information to others, whether you're working alone or in a team. A coach who tells his top player that his batting average needs to increase is communicating to the rest of the team that work needs to be done and what should be improved. Your colleagues will be informed of what has to happen, when, and why by your internally stated goals.

It Serves as a Measuring Stick

Although it may seem obvious, the player and the squad needed a mechanism to determine "success" after all their tireless work. In the instance of our player, it was a puzzling statistic that indicates a more serious issue. The team's comprehension of the outcomes of his labor was immediately improved by having a metric by which to gauge progress.

It Helps by Recognizing Progress

In addition, when the journey from point A to point B goes on, weary bodies and dwindling enthusiasm can result. Having these more manageable objectives along the road gives everyone a reason to celebrate and acknowledge a job well done. Since achieving aspirations can take years, celebrating small successes can help create momentum for major successes.

Goals Help You Prioritize

Determining what's significant involves creating expectations for each component of your endeavor. Choosing where to start and where to make the largest impact is the most critical because you can only work on one goal at a time. Consider how one goal affects the other. Concentrate on what will truly matter, and remember that achieving one objective will help you achieve others.

Targets Make You Accountable

Our player starts developing his mental toughness at this point. He records his performances in a journal, listens to loud music while in the batting cage, and makes notes of his mental state when things are difficult so that he can make corrections. His statistics finally start to rise, and the team starts to succeed.

This drive to adapt and all of the additional practice came from a clearly stated expectation. Setting a target for that particular player meant that, should he not develop, the team may alter his focus or decide on his future with the team. Although it can be difficult to admit failure, it is important to understand what failure is and what success is to analyze your aims and the strategies you employed to achieve them.

Monitoring Progress Is Vital

Big, ambitious goals like a prevalent social presence or a world championship are admirable (and essential), but even the best-set plans can go off course halfway if they are not carefully observed. Tracking your progress and periodically re-evaluating your tactics, strategy, and effort will help you stay on track because even personal aspirations that originally appear reasonable may lead you astray.

Goals Guide Actions

Let's now apply the aforementioned comparison to your project or the criteria you're using to assess your success. It's crucial to assess your team and see how each component may be improved because you'll need to take action in order to advance toward your definition of success. You may decide what has to be done, if anything, about each component of your intent by creating goals.

It's Essential to Define Success

Our illustration highlights a further advantage of goal-setting: the definition of success. Our player succeeds on his own. But even if he hits the most home runs in a season, his team isn't doing well. As a result, we set the playoffs as our aim, and the player's role immediately changes. Knowing what you want to achieve and how your goals can help you get there in addition to shaping individual efforts steers the entire team in the same direction.

It will be easier to get things going or turn around a failing team if you know what success looks like for you and create benchmarks for achieving it. Understanding your priorities and end goal will help you articulate them and inspire change. Utilize the common target of your team to achieve little triumphs and act with purpose based on the appropriate criteria. When the trophy is ultimately raised, this shared desire, momentum, and achievement, will mean more than you can imagine. However, doing so will require some organization and a small break in your efforts.

Setting Realistic and Achievable Goals

A realistic goal is one that you can accomplish based on your abilities, timescale, and level of motivation. But you won't come any closer to reaching these targets until you decide what they are.

You should still consider realistic aims as something you can achieve even though what is practical for one person may not be realistic for another. You must, above all, have faith in your goals. You cannot honestly consider them to be aspirations if you don't believe in them from the beginning.

Set Milestones

Goals require deadlines... as we've seen before. However, it's equally crucial to establish certain checkpoints along the way. You may set a milestone at the end of each year, for instance, if your target will take five years to complete. You can check to see if your action plan is working as intended in this manner.

Setting milestones can also fuel your motivation, which will undoubtedly grow as you observe your success!

Avoid Comparing Your Journey to Others

Your targets might not be unique, but you, your environment, and your resources are. Therefore, never compare yourself to others, even if it might be inspiring to have someone who you're working to achieve a certain goal.

You may lose motivation if you believe you fall short of your targets or you may get overconfident if you believe you are currently closer to accomplishing them than anybody else. Your journey is special, personal, and unlike anybody else's.

Share Your Aspirations

We often get told that sharing our goals with someone holds us accountable. This is true in most cases. However, we should share our dreams with someone we admire. Sharing your ambitions with a higher-up not only holds you accountable but also raises motivation.

The reason is simple—you are concerned about what this person thinks of you and end up with a resolve to make them proud.

Expect Failure

Expect the best but brace yourself for the worst. While believing in yourself and your ability is critical, it is also essential to be prepared to fail. It is unavoidable and will occur sooner or later. So, be ready and alter your expectations.

You may not have completed all of your objectives, but it does not imply you will not achieve your ultimate aim. If and when you fail, just get back up and resume working toward your major goal. A healthy dose of realism and enthusiasm is always the best option!

Breaking Down Long-Term Goals Into Short-Term Steps

Long-term goals require effort to achieve, which means that they can seem intimidating at first. This is when short-term objectives come into play. These smaller stepping stones divide the labor into bite-sized tasks that may be completed in a shorter period, such as a day, week, or month.

To set short-term objectives, list all of the actions that must be completed to achieve your long-term target. Consider them dependencies—achieving these goals frees up space for your ultimate, long-term ambition. Then, transform each of those dependents into a separate objective.

For example, suppose your team has established a long-term goal of developing a new customer service process within the next six months. You could do it in the following steps:

- Collect feedback and ideas from the customer service personnel this week.

- This month, evaluate the present process and identify areas for improvement.

- Collect client input and discover prevalent problem issues in two months.

- Submit a business case to executive stakeholders that outlines your suggested modifications in three months.

- Finish your project plan in four months.

- Train customer service personnel in the new processes in five months.

- Roll out the new methodology to all customer service teams in six months.

See how breaking a larger goal makes achieving it easier? Don't try to eat the whole cake with one bite. Slice it into pieces. As a result, you may just find others who are willing (and deserving) to eat a few slices with you.

Everyday Habits to Achieving Your Goals

According to research, 45% of Americans typically make New Year's resolutions, but only 8% of them are genuinely accomplished (Halvorson, 2015). What is it that distinguishes those 8% so much? It may seem straightforward, yet it all boils down to their habits.

Let's talk about the habits of people who are set on achieving their goals.

Make Being Healthy a Habit

Although being in shape might seem like a goal in and of itself, it eventually aids in the achievement of your other goals. Those that are successful appear to have boundless vitality, a feat which they accomplish by maintaining a healthy diet and keeping themselves active. You give yourself the best chance of success by making healthy decisions. And yes, deciding to be healthy may require quite a bit of self-discipline, but still, the rewards are boundless.

Pull Out the Weeds and Plant Flowers

Setting a goal to do something new is far more beneficial than setting a goal to quit doing something. If you want to break a poor habit, concentrate on developing a new behavior for that circumstance. Instead of saying, "I'll never show anger toward my boss," a particular, constructive habit would be something like, "When I feel angry at my boss, I'll take 10 seconds before responding."

Acknowledge That All Qualities Can Improve

Because they believe they aren't capable of achieving their goals, some people become demoralized and give up. Those who succeed, understand that this is untrue; even intelligence or personality can develop with time. You'll flourish with greater efficiency if you make it a habit to improve all of your traits. Similarly, never believe that you are *perfect* and don't need improvement. That is the character of a fixed mindset, which will not get you anywhere.

Specify Your Goals

Unfortunately, lacking a clear finish line is one of the things that prevents many goal-setters from succeeding. "I want to lose weight" is a general goal; is losing one pound considered a success? Instead, those who consistently achieve their goals tend to be very clear about what they intend to do, such as "I want to lose 15 pounds in three months."

Be Altruistic

It's crucial to keep up motivation when a goal's path becomes challenging. Those that are successful in accomplishing their targets set significant accomplishments as their benchmarks. They frequently concentrate on aims that aid others. It's simpler to keep pushing in the direction of success when you're aware that you're doing good.

List Your Targets

Successful people have a strong practice of keeping a written record of every goal they set and the date it was attained. In addition to giving them a track record to build on, this makes the aim seem more achievable.

Set Smaller Objectives on the Way to the Final Target

Many people begin with lofty goals that motivate them but are, regrettably, difficult to achieve. It's essential to divide large goals into smaller milestone objectives so that you can monitor your progress and maintain motivation as you move toward them.

Stop Making Excuses

When they don't succeed, many people end up finding justifications. Successful people don't hide behind excuses; rather, they view failures as an opportunity to re-evaluate and try again. Make it a habit to resist giving in to justifications and instead empower yourself to continue working toward your aim.

Make It a Habit to Persevere

The adage "When the going gets tough, the tough get going" is a way of life for individuals who routinely succeed in their aims. They mentally get ready to push through by acknowledging how challenging the road to their aspirations will be. If you want to be someone who achieves their goals, having the habit of endurance is key.

Make Time to Work on Your Targets

Successful people are aware that time does not carve itself. They set aside specified time to work on an endeavor when they are committed to achieving it and treat this time with the same respect as if they were meeting with clients. You'll always succeed if you develop the habit of scheduling time to work on your goals.

Be Humble About Your Skills

The people who are most successful in achieving their goals are aware that there is always room for improvement. They can embrace assistance and repeatedly achieve success by being humble and teachable.

Utilizing the power of habit rather than possessing superhuman strength will help you achieve your goals consistently. You'll be considerably more likely to consistently achieve your targets if you adopt these habits.

As was mentioned in this chapter, successful goal-setting and achievement are only made possible with proper time management. We'll explore this skill in the next chapter.

Chapter 5: Managing Time and Prioritizing Tasks

Coordination of duties and activities maximizes the impact of a person's efforts through time management. In essence, time management is used to help people complete more tasks and work efficiently.

To make the most of the time available, time-management techniques include organization, planning, and scheduling. Techniques for time management also take into account a person's unique circumstance as well as any applicable skills and traits.

There are certain "barriers" that negatively affect effective time management. These barriers can either be internal or external. Internal barriers are specific to the individual and can therefore be overcome by the affected person. External barriers have to do with the individual's circumstances, and therefore, cannot be changed by the affected person.

Examples of internal barriers include:

- lack of motivation

- multitasking

- people pleasing

- lack of self-control

Some examples of external barriers include:

- a lack of corporate resources

- a heavy workload

- distractions

- job constraints

While the individual likely can't do anything to change these external barriers, they can still decide how they will react to and deal with them. Let's explore how one can overcome these barriers.

Understanding the Importance of Time Management

The value of time management lies in its capacity to give time purpose and enable individuals to maximize it well. It is used in the corporate world to establish objectives and standards for organizations and the people who work for them. Employees with efficient time-management skills can produce high-quality work and accomplish their objectives. Time management also assists managers in identifying employee potential and establishing practical objectives.

Employees with poor time-management abilities are likely to miss deadlines, produce subpar work, experience excessive tension and anxiety, and usually run out of time. Ineffective time management negatively impacts staff, management, and the business.

Poor or absent time management leads to time poverty, when there is too much to accomplish and not enough time to complete it. Despite working hard, their personal life suffers and they feel increasingly overburdened with obligations and activities.

Making deliberate decisions about one's priorities is necessary for time management. Without time management, people constantly respond to outside stimuli and feel out of control in their jobs and personal life.

Even though all work requires time, some activities are more important than others. Both productivity and work-life balance are improved by reallocating time to higher-value tasks. An overall healthier workplace is created by effective time management.

This practice has benefits for both the company and its personnel. These are some of the advantages:

- **Improved Reputation:** Businesses that promote efficient time management are regarded as desirable workplaces, which enhances employee attraction and retention.

- **Fewer Turnovers:** Employees are more inclined to stay at a job and not go elsewhere when they have a better work experience.

- **Increased Creativity:** Employees can be more creative in their job when they are not under pressure from time restraints. Instead of simply responding to their work, they can actively engage with it. This fosters creativity.

- **Improvements in Productivity:** Employees who enjoy their jobs and are less inclined to be absent are more productive.

- **Reduced Absenteeism:** Employees that are stressed and exhausted take more sick days and other vacations.

- **Happier Employees:** Employees are happier and less likely to experience burnout when they have ample time to do their work.

Now that we have covered its importance, let's look at setting priorities, which is one of the most important aspects of time management.

Setting Priorities and Making the Most of Your Time

In order to perform activities in the right order, one should rank them according to their importance. You might be able to better manage your time with this technique. This teaches you how to finish highly important tasks first so that you may meet deadlines and have more time for bigger tasks. Your ability to prioritize tasks will enable you to complete more work in less time.

How to Prioritize Tasks in the Workplace

When setting task priorities at work, take the following steps into account:

First Determine Which Tasks Are Most Crucial

Find the items on your to-do list that are the most important. This could be decided based on upcoming deadlines, client demands, or requests from coworkers. For instance, before tackling other duties, you can concentrate on a marketing report that is due at the end of the day.

Second, Create a Calendar Containing Your Tasks

Schedule the duties on your calendar after deciding which ones are most essential. When you view your daily job list, setting priorities can be simpler. When you have a visible reminder of every daily activity you need to perform, you may find that you can concentrate better on them. A sense of accomplishment can also be gained from completing them.

Third, Establish Boundaries

After focusing on your daily tasks, you can further prioritize your tasks by designating certain times to work. Coworkers may routinely walk over to your desk, call, or email you to discuss non-urgent matters; therefore, telling them that you are working on a project and will chat with them later is appropriate. You can let them know that you'd prefer to talk in the afternoon but don't want to be disturbed in the morning.

Setting your "away" email message to inform people of the times of day you respond to emails is another strategy to prioritize your time. When you schedule particular times to work without interruptions, you could discover that you focus better and complete more things.

Prioritize Each Job Individually

Although multitasking may seem like a good way to get more done, it is frequently preferable to concentrate on one job at a time. By using this technique, you can make sure that assignment has all of your focus so that you may finish it quickly before moving on to the next item on your list. You stand a better chance of producing high-quality work when your attention isn't diverted by other duties.

Delegate Duties

You could create a list of everything you need to accomplish by the end of the week and allocate particular tasks to others if you are able to delegate duties or share responsibility with coworkers. To free up your time to focus on matters that require your immediate attention, decide which responsibilities your coworkers could complete without your supervision and assign those tasks to them. You can prioritize the tasks that need to be completed as soon as possible using this method.

Enlist the Aid of Technology

With technological improvements, there are many productivity tools available that can assist you in setting priorities and maintaining focus. You may monitor how productively you're working by downloading an application to your computer that tracks the time you spend on a certain job. A timer can also be used to focus on work and schedule breaks. You may, for instance, set your timer for an hour of work and decide to take a five-minute break after that.

Utilize a Scheduling Tool

Write down every task that is due within the next month to help you prioritize. Next, decide what must be accomplished every day, at the end of every week, and by the end of the month. This can be recorded on a spreadsheet, and the tasks can then be set up on a calendar. Setting deadlines for your projects helps keep you focused and increases your productivity.

Managing Distractions and Staying Focused

It takes time and effort to learn how to maintain your focus at work. However, you may reduce both physical and digital distractions by using some simple strategies.

Here are a few suggestions:

Don't Be Tempted by Your Smartphone

We consume content unrelated to our jobs for a significant portion of each day on our mobile devices. And in some ways, it was planned that way. Your material never ends because of the endless scrolling in your LinkedIn newsfeed. Your brain lacks cues to quit reading because there aren't any apparent stops.

You may lessen how distracting your smartphone is by doing the following:

Turn Off as Many Notifications as You Can

The "Do Not Disturb" setting on your phone will stop it from buzzing. You can set up your phone to accept important calls and texts from specific people if you're worried about emergencies.

Blocking Distracting Apps From Appearing on Your Home Screen

If they are not the first thing you see, you will be less inclined to use them. Your favorite apps can be moved to a different page or completely removed from the app display.

Converting the Screen to Grayscale

Red notification badges and vibrant logos are how apps clamor for your attention. On a black and white screen, their allure is muted.

Set a Limited Time for Correspondence

If you let it, checking your emails and texts may take over your entire day. Consider disabling your push alerts and only checking your messages during specific times of the day. If it genuinely is urgent, they'll find another way to get in touch with you.

Clarify Your Priorities

Set key jobs in order of importance, then pick one or two to finish. Even if you didn't do the little things on your list, you can sleep better knowing the urgent work is finished.

Take Breaks

Working a lot of hours can be exhausting. Your body will take a break if you don't schedule one for yourself. During lulls, wander about, stretch, chat with people, or sip tea. Making time for rest will enable you to unwind at your own pace and maintain focus when it's needed.

Create Records

Keep a log of the tasks you do at work and when distractions occur. A pattern will eventually appear, and you'll discover how to anticipate potential disruptions. For instance, if your supervisor wants a progress report every afternoon, try delivering it early. You'll have more control over your schedule and working conditions when you complete activities like this on your own terms.

Everyday Habits to Managing Your Time

The key to effective time management is working smarter, instead of simply harder. Try out different strategies from this list to determine which ones work best for you. In time, they will develop into habits.

Create a Task Plan for Tomorrow

Plan the things you need to complete the following day and how long they will each take at the end of each day. After that, block off those chores on your calendar between the existing appointments. Mindset management is the key to effective time management. Your professional and personal lives will become less stressful once you know that you are in charge of your clock and can decide what to do with each passing hour.

Make a List of "5 Before 11"

List five tasks you can complete before 11 a.m. of the following day on your "5 before 11" list. Does each task advance your priorities, purposes, and objectives? It ought to. You'll feel incredibly serene and accomplished after you complete your five-before-eleven tasks, knowing that you've done something important.

Be the Early Bird

Set an earlier alarm than everyone else. When you study the biographies and memoirs of successful people, you'll notice that practically all of them share the practice of going to bed at a decent hour and rising early.

You can organize your day in advance and begin working on some duties that may be hanging over your head by rising before the rest of the world so that you don't have to deal with interruptions from others.

Include Unstructured Time in Your Schedule

Include two to four hours of free time per week in your schedule. This time has been set apart for the sole purpose of thinking, learning, and exploring. This may appear illogical or downright unreasonable to many busy business owners, but two aspects support the value of scheduling "slack" time:

- Your brain's bandwidth is maxed out when you are continually occupied and have no free time, as in when every minute of every day is scheduled back-to-back. As a result, your cognitive abilities weaken, you are more prone to mistakes, and you are less analytical.

- Jeff Bezos left his Mondays and Thursdays fully unscheduled when he first started at Amazon so that he would always have time to reflect deeply on the company's vision (Keenan, 2022). Viewing unstructured time as essential is a trait of successful CEOs because without it, they will constantly be responding to the issues people bring to their attention and never planning ahead for the company's future.

Understand the Importance of Being Organized

Staying organized is an essential time-management strategy. Our capacity to focus and concentrate is impaired by excessive clutter and disorder. Maintaining mental organization is equally as important as having your surroundings physically organized.

Establish a Time Limit for Tasks

Take your project or work product and divide it into smaller subtasks. Set up time monitoring or determine how long it will take to complete each of those activities, even if they just take five minutes each.

Therefore, be extremely specific about what you want to do so that you can tick things off your list when you're finished and get that dopamine rush that will keep you inspired, motivated, and thrilled to keep working. If we don't, we often wake up and start working without thinking, and we labor for hours on end without ever feeling like we've achieved what we set out to.

Delegate if Possible

If possible, get a skilled assistant who you can trust to handle basic tasks like scheduling. An assistant may be one of your best resources for increasing productivity and lowering stress.

Be Realistic With Time Allocation

Freely allot the time required to complete the bare minimum of the following step of a task. In other words, something that will contribute to achieving your short-term objective. Be realistic—don't plan according to how long you want to take, but how long it would actually take. Once you've made that choice, just get to work without giving it a second thought.

Ironically, some people spend a lot of time thinking about time management, which is an enormous time waster! They are not giving their tasks or problems their full focus because they are preoccupied with how long something takes. While it's good to think about and know how long something should take, it's not efficient to obsess about it.

Also, allow yourself to feel free from guilt. Don't feel rushed to complete something—you won't need to if your allocated times are realistic.

When Stuck, Seek Something Simple

Allow yourself to complete the simplest and smallest portion of the task if you become stuck, are unsure how to begin a project, become anxious, or begin to procrastinate. Reduce your objective from finishing the entire project to completing the easiest, most manageable part, such as writing the first sentence, adding the first line of code, or creating the first row in the spreadsheet.

What usually happens is that, after completing the first task, it spills over into the next and then the next, and like a snowball, hours later you are rushing downhill, forgetting even why it was so difficult to begin with.

Pause and Reflect

Stopping everything and taking a moment to reflect is one of the most essential things a successful person can do.

Contemplate your day for at least five minutes in the morning:

- What are you most eager to get done today?

- Do you have that priority listed on your timetable?

Set your phone to chime hourly and think about the following:

- Am I doing what I should be doing?

- Is this who I most want to be?

After the day, take five minutes to reflect and ask yourself:

- What did I discover? Is there anyone I need to recognize or thank?

- Do I want to change anything for tomorrow?

Effectiveness, working on what's most important, and ignoring everything else (for the time being) are the keys to proper time management.

Regularly Purge Your Mind of Clutter

You're under pressure because you have a lot of remaining tasks. List each one on a blank sheet of paper. Any that are not absolutely necessary can then be crossed out. Be ruthless! As you look over your list, resolve to cross off one item per day until it is finished. Check this list frequently!

Take It Slow

Maybe you're constantly in over-performance mode because you're all invested. Take it slow. Time is available. You'll need patience, energy, and focus; if you launch into high gear straight away, you'll be more likely to exhaust yourself.

For each of the tasks on your list, do you know what constitutes good enough? Do what is right and acceptable. Overanalyzing, over-editing, and over-tweaking are unnecessary time wasters. Do good work, then put it to rest.

Group Related Tasks

Take some time to go over the complete list rather than starting at the top and working your way down. Then, group related tasks together. You might classify your activities into categories like phone calls, money, networking, paperwork, or artistic endeavors.

Your brain can avoid switching between different types of thought by grouping (or batching) activities that are similar in character. This ensures that smoother transitions are achieved. As you complete related tasks, you acquire momentum and, in certain cases, even speed up!

Conduct a Time Audit

Understanding how your time is spent will help you make better use of it. There are excellent time-tracking apps available.

Alternatively, list your primary tasks for the day on a straightforward three-by-five notecard. Because the workday always manages to sneak in lots of extras, you should list any tasks you completed that you had not originally planned to complete on the back of the card.

You can check what you prioritized (and if you completed it) by looking at your three-by-five card at the end of the day. You can also see what tasks were added to your to-do list. Extra work is acceptable, but if your daily major tasks aren't getting completed, there's a problem.

Time management often requires toughness and perseverance, and most of all, self-discipline. A great way to become mentally stronger is by building resilience, which we will discuss in the next chapter.

Chapter 6: Building Resilience and Overcoming Challenges

After finding the wishing well, do you think Ben and Charlie were able to develop resilience? Likely not, right? Resilience is built on the hardships of life.

Being resilient means being able to adjust to life's setbacks and tragedies. How well do you recover from setbacks? Do you tend to fall apart? Are you able to find empowerment when things are tough?

When you are resilient, you are able to draw on your inner strength to overcome obstacles or setbacks such as losing your job, being sick, experiencing a tragedy, or losing a loved one. A lack of resilience can cause you to dwell on issues, feel victimized, become overwhelmed, or use unhealthy coping methods such as eating disorders, substance abuse, or dangerous behaviors.

While resilience won't make your challenges disappear, it can help you rediscover happiness in life, see past your troubles, and cope with stress more effectively. You can learn to increase your resilience if it isn't as strong as you'd like it to be.

Understanding Resilience

The ability to successfully adjust to severe or hard life circumstances is referred to as resilience. Being able to adapt to both internal and external demands requires flexibility in one's thinking, feeling, and conduct.

According to Amit Sood, MD, the executive director of the Global Center for Resiliency and Well-Being and the developer of the Resilient Option program, "It's your ability to withstand adversity, bounce back, and grow despite life's downturns" (Hurley, 2022).

It's important to remember that developing your skill set to become resilient over time is essential. You must put in the effort to develop resilience, and you'll probably encounter obstacles along the way.

It depends on your own actions and abilities (such as communication and self-esteem), as well as on external factors (like your social network and the resources you have access to). Even those who are resilient go through stress, emotional turmoil, and pain. Working through emotional pain and suffering is a sign of resilience.

Resilience, as explained by Dr. Sood, incorporates these five principles:

- gratitude

- compassion

- acceptance

- meaning

- forgiveness

People that are resilient are better able to emotionally withstand trauma, adversity, and hardship. They make use of their resources, talents, and strengths to overcome obstacles and recover from failures.

Relying on unhealthy coping mechanisms (including avoidance, isolation, and self-medication) is more common in those lacking in resilience since they are more prone to feel overwhelmed or powerless. Greater overall well-being and life satisfaction are more likely to be experienced by individuals with resilience, coping skills, and emotional intelligence than by those with less resilience.

The **7 Cs model of resilience** was created by Ken Ginsburg, MD, a co-founder of the Center for Parent and Teen Communication and a pediatrician at the Children's Hospital of Philadelphia (Hurley, 2022).

These are the **7 Cs**:

Coping: People who develop excellent coping mechanisms for stress are better equipped to deal with difficulty and setbacks.

Character: To make moral decisions, contribute to society, and feel worthy of themselves, people need a basic understanding of right and wrong.

Competence: This is the capacity to recognize how to address circumstances successfully. People acquire a set of abilities that will enable them to trust their judgment and make ethical decisions as they increase their competence.

Confidence: Competence is the foundation of genuine self-confidence. By showcasing their skill in everyday settings, people build their confidence.

Control: Understanding internal control enables people to address problems instead of acting as victims of circumstance. People are more inclined to regard themselves as capable and confident when they realize that they have influence over the results of their decisions.

Contribution: A sense of purpose is a strong motivator. Giving back to one's community strengthens reciprocal bonds.

Connection: A sense of security and belonging is provided through close links to family, friends, and the community.

Although the term "resilience" is frequently used to refer to general adaptability and coping, it can further be understood by exploring its four categories.

Emotional Resilience

Everybody handles stress and adversity on a different emotional level. Some people are more or less susceptible to change by nature. While some may experience a wave of emotions in response to a circumstance, others may not.

Emotionally resilient people are aware of their feelings and their causes. Even in times of crisis, they maintain a sense of realistic optimism and take the initiative to use both internal and external resources to survive. They are competent at effectively controlling both their own emotions and outside stimuli.

Community Resilience

The ability of a community to respond to and recover from challenging circumstances, such as natural disasters, violent crimes, economic difficulties, and other issues that affect the community as a whole, is referred to as community resilience.

Examples of communities that have recovered from disasters and tragedies include New York City after the 9/11 terrorist attacks and New Orleans after Hurricane Katrina. America's resilience was put to the test like never before with the COVID-19 epidemic, an unparalleled public health emergency.

Psychological Resilience

The capacity to mentally cope with or adapt to uncertainties, difficulties, and adversity is known as psychological resilience. Another term for it is "mental fortitude."

Psychologically resilient people learn coping mechanisms and abilities that allow them to remain composed and on task throughout a crisis and recover without suffering anguish or anxiety over the long run.

Physical Resilience

Physical resiliency is the body's capacity to overcome obstacles, keep its strength and endurance, and heal swiftly and effectively. It refers to a person's capacity to carry out daily activities and bounce back after accidents, illnesses, or other physical demands.

As people experience physical pressures and medical concerns, physical resilience is vital to good aging. It is influenced by a variety of factors, including healthy lifestyle choices, relationships with friends and neighbors, deep breathing, wise rest and recovery time, and participation in enjoyable activities.

Building Resilience in Daily Life

Resilience is a skill that can be learned and maintained in both personal and professional contexts, despite the fact that people respond to stress in various ways. By raising our levels of resilience, we develop greater mental and emotional flexibility and, as a result, learn to adapt and deal with stress more effectively.

To help you become more resilient on a daily basis, try some of these suggestions.

Don't Lose Sight

Try to keep your long-term goals in mind and keep the stressful issue in context, even while dealing with really challenging situations. Be careful not to overestimate the situation.

Be Adaptable

Learn to compromise with your coworkers, family, and friends as a start. The sooner you realize there are other options besides your path, the sooner you will understand how to handle a difficult situation. It's possible that rigid thinking was what initially put you in that stressful position.

Accept Change as Part of Life

Recognize that adapting to change is a necessary component of daily living. Unfavorable circumstances may make some goals no longer reachable. Focusing on the situations that you can change will be made easier by accepting the circumstances that cannot be changed.

Do Something!

Act decisively rather than hoping issues will go away. Don't allow your problems to paralyze you to the point of inaction or inertia. Even if it's just a tiny step, move forward by taking any action necessary and relevant.

Recognize Setbacks as Temporary

Maintain a long-term focus on the future and try not to consider crises as impassable obstacles. Although extremely stressful circumstances may be inevitable, you can change how you perceive them and react to them. Consider how things might be a little better in the future by thinking beyond the immediate situation. As you navigate challenging circumstances, take note of any small ways in which you could already feel more at ease.

Find Opportunities for Self-Discovery

People often discover something about themselves and may find that they have improved in some way as a result of their loss-related struggles. Numerous people who have gone through disasters and adversity have reported better relationships, a stronger sense of self-worth despite feeling vulnerable, a deeper sense of strength, and a greater respect for life following their ordeal.

Set Achievable Goals

Although goals were discussed in Chapter 4, setting achievable goals is still relevant to developing resilience. Even if it feels like a minor accomplishment, keep your attention on tiny steps and doable, frequent objectives. You can achieve your ultimate goals with the aid of these. Rather than concentrating on targets that seem unreachable, ask yourself: *What's one thing I know I can achieve today that will help me advance in the direction I want to go?*

You Matter

Be mindful of your own needs and emotions. Take part in peaceful and enjoyable activities, and exercise frequently. Taking care of yourself keeps your body and mind prepared to handle challenges that call for resilience. Not only do these activities help you unwind after a stressful day, but they also help you become more resilient to stress in the future.

If Necessary, Seek Professional Help

It takes patience and practice to become more resilient. Consider speaking to a mental health professional if you don't feel like you're making progress or if you don't know where to begin. With help, you can strengthen your mental health and resilience.

Resilience ultimately involves seeing difficult circumstances as opportunities to develop your character and advance as a person. Stress strengthens your character and sharpens your problem-solving skills. Thus, you'll be able to appreciate life more, take pleasure in challenges, and get through obstructions that only momentarily stand in your way if you learn to live with and manage stress. In short, you can see stress as an opportunity.

Overcoming Adversity and Setbacks

Setbacks are unforeseen events that tend to happen when we least expect them in our lives. They may arise in our personal lives as a result of a family member's passing, a divorce, or challenging health circumstances. Or, in our professional lives as a result of job cuts, layoffs, or a negative performance review.

Nevertheless, most people will encounter setbacks at various times throughout their life. The issue is not *if* but rather *when* the setback will happen. Unfortunately, setbacks frequently occur when you are least prepared, so plan accordingly.

It's crucial to first realize that a setback is just momentary. Despite the intense feelings you may be experiencing, this is not a permanent situation. People can make poor decisions or feel despondent as a result of the emotions that they experience after suffering a setback.

Without a solid support network, a person could fall into a dark place where their judgment, clarity, or behaviors are affected. It is critical to surround yourself with people who value your potential, are aware of your circumstances, and who will support you while you face the challenges of the setback. This might be a work colleague, a relative, or a qualified coach. You'll be able to better understand yourself as a result.

You are already aware of your passions, limitations, and strengths. Therefore, consider your approach to setbacks. What is your response to them? How do you treat others? How do you make other people feel while handling a setback? How do you interact with those nearby? Knowing yourself and what you require in these circumstances is the first step toward overcoming hardship. You can use this information to play to your strengths.

Reverting to your roots is a good option when you're faced with challenging circumstances. This enables you to capitalize on your strengths. Everybody is born with specific aptitudes. We often take our power for granted since it comes naturally to us. Ask your coworkers, friends, and family members who spend the most time with you if you aren't sure what it is. Hearing the same responses from individuals who know you best may surprise you.

It's crucial to capitalize on your strengths when you experience difficulties. By building on your abilities, you can earn success and boost your confidence, which may decline after a loss. Utilizing your strengths helps you become more confident and less likely to take failure personally.

Avoid wasting time blaming others and focusing on what went wrong. Don't waste your precious time thinking about who wronged you or how unfair life is. Once you have a clear understanding of what transpired, it's time to regroup and move on. Instead, take advantage of the chance to reinvent yourself. Setbacks often help us realize how tenacious we are. You are stronger than you realize. You can have the insight you need to create a plan if you don't take the failure personally.

Everyday Habits to Build Resilience and Overcoming Challenges

It is not a hereditary inclination, but rather a skill, to be able to handle challenging circumstances at work or home. In this regard, developing resilience is similar to mastering any skill and will greatly improve the quality of your life.

There are always issues to face in life, thus it makes sense to train yourself to be intellectually strong and fit. This is something that can be enhanced by developing daily routines and practices.

Give Yourself Some Love

Resilient people are kinder to themselves and have a wider tolerance range. People who suffer, commonly tend to blame themselves and think they are worthless. That only intensifies the distress and makes coping more difficult. While accepting responsibility is important, there is no use in punishing yourself in any situation.

Create and Develop Routines

Every day, the brain analyzes countless emotions and behaviors. Creating routines will aid in establishing order, lowering stress levels, and reducing the strain on our finite supply of motivation, which dwindles over time. Let's look at some examples.

Morning Routine: Ideally, rising naturally and beginning the day with some activities like working out, stretching, and organizing the day. Additionally, activities like reading, journaling, and meditation can be taken into account.

Evening Routine: Use a de-energize hour to prepare for a good night's sleep by turning off all electronic devices (including your tablet, laptop, and smartphone) an hour before bed. Take a warm shower after that to elevate and then drop your body temperature. The final 20 minutes are for relaxation. Try reading, meditating, or deep breathing; you'll fall asleep in a few minutes when you switch off the light. After a restful night's quality sleep, life seems amazingly different.

Speaking of Sleep

Every organ system in the body is impacted by sleep. When you're fatigued, you're more likely to eat poorly and have less motivation to exercise. Additionally, sleep has a significant impact on our mood and social interactions.

A good night's sleep depends on a variety of elements and is a process that must be mastered. Before going to bed, establish a daily routine; such as what was mentioned in the previous point.

Keep Challenges in Perspective

If you are facing a challenge, think about how serious the issue will be in a day, a week, a month, or a year, if ignored. This method enables people to realize that, for most of us, our current issues will have minimal bearing on us a year from now.

Resilient people can comfort themselves that although the situation may not be ideal right now, it probably won't last forever. This is partly about perspective, but it's also about being able to identify the unpleasant emotions brought on by stressful circumstances while keeping things in perspective and understanding that these feelings will pass.

A Mindset of Gratitude

Not only is gratitude a behavior, but it is also a feeling that has physiological benefits. Consequently, gratitude is more than just being grateful; it is a deeper appreciation for someone or something that results in happier emotions that lasts longer.

Consider everyday mishaps like spilled drinks or computer glitches as opportunities to practice optimism. Think about this: how long will it last? Just how awful is it? How much will I blame myself for? You can develop resilience as a habit by consistently practicing this attitude.

Improve Your Physical Health

Eat healthy food and engage in regular physical activity. Drink more water to make sure you're hydrated. Being physically healthy will boost your energy levels, as well as your mood and overall well-being. This will also aid in your efforts to strengthen your resilience.

Define Your Purpose

This is about having a wider point of view. What are your goals for your life, your why, and your purpose? Think about waking up each morning with the specific goal of enjoying your day. Consolidate this by setting daily and weekly goals to help you stay motivated.

Additionally, having an understanding of the bigger picture often allows one to put daily issues into perspective and makes them appear a little easier.

Meditating for Resilience

We have discussed meditation before, such as in Chapter 2, but it is also relevant and beneficial when it comes to building resilience.

But how? Your mental health and overall well-being will be significantly improved by the powerful practice of meditation. These are a few advantages:

- It enables you to keep your focus on the here and now.

- It aids in developing stress management skills.

- It fosters creativity and inventiveness.

- It helps by lowering negative feelings.

- It enables you to view challenging circumstances from a fresh angle.

- It encourages tolerance and patience.

Establish Strong Relationships

Those who are most resilient are also the best at asking for assistance. They realize they can't make it on their own. Remember that no one can accomplish everything by themselves all the time, not even the best, strongest, and most resilient individuals.

Maintaining relationships and sharing positive experiences with those closest to us are essential. People are social beings, something that may easily be taken for granted. Our happiness as well as our health and well-being will be positively impacted by strong relationships.

Resilience is a key element of self-discipline. Without it, we will be tossed around like the waves of the sea, making being disciplined more challenging. However, to endure building resilience, it will help a great deal to be motivated. In the next chapter, we'll talk about motivation, and how to remain focused and positive.

Chapter 7: Staying Focused and Motivated

Life is full of surprises—some we like and some we don't. It's easy to get sidetracked and lose perspective. Being demotivated is like trying to drive a car with flat wheels: you won't get far. Focus and motivation work together—Feeling motivated sharpens your focus. Achieving success because of your focus inspires motivation. This is how they feed each other positive energy.

However, if you lack motivation, it can have a detrimental impact on your focus, and vice versa. Let's discuss how you can live a life of success based on laser-sharp focus and endless motivation.

Maintaining Focus and Motivation

Maybe this sounds familiar: You're trying to focus on the massive project that is due on Friday, but it's already 3 p.m. and a Wednesday. The pressure is on, but it's getting harder to keep on task, and you may be feeling frustrated or overwhelmed.

Fortunately, there are methods for staying motivated and focused that don't involve drinking eight cups of coffee or, as most people do, criticizing ourselves. Here are some suggestions for boosting motivation and sharpening your focus if you often feel scattered and unfocused.

Determine Your Motivation First

To determine what drives you, consider the big picture. It's easy to lose sight of the bigger picture while dealing with a large task or a tight deadline. Consider asking yourself again, "Why am I doing this?" Your response may help you rediscover what truly motivates you and return to your work with a fresh sense of purpose.

Going back to the beginning and discovering what makes you excited and why can help you stay motivated. Many leaders rely on "autonomous forms of regulation," which means they are motivated by their inner principles rather than by guilt or fear to maintain their motivation (Tsuei, 2021).

We all have different things that drive us, but it usually comes down to one or more of the following: long-term professional goals, a supportive team, people you care about, or a job that makes you feel completely fulfilled.

Schedule Time Blocks for Work That Demand High Focus

Should you decide to accept it, the objective is to enter a flow state, which is a state in which you are "in the flow" or so engaged with the work at hand that both place and time fade. Even though the work or activity itself may be tough or challenging, focusing on it becomes second nature. It's crucial to understand that entering a flow state cannot be forced. However, there are steps you can take to increase the likelihood that flow will occur. Let's explore a few of them.

Allow Yourself Enough Time to Zone In

Focus and motivation suffer when they are simultaneously pushed in five different directions. If you just have 10 minutes here and there to finish work, it's challenging to get into the flow. A capable calendar assistant can help you identify those important time slots and create the environment necessary for creativity. To make time for focused work, some available apps will automatically group your meetings and other responsibilities. Focus can be maintained by managing your time.

Keep Your Eye on the End Goal

Take it easy on yourself. You are most certainly not alone if you are currently having trouble keeping motivated and focused. Do not forget to look after yourself. Maintaining good mental health at work takes time, so drink plenty of water and don't be shy about seeking assistance if you need to.

Take a Breather When You're Feeling Stressed Out or Disorganized

To prevent burnout, remember to take breaks whenever you feel frazzled or overloaded. Consider taking a little pause during your workday to stretch, get a sparkling drink from the fridge, or otherwise move your body rather than pushing through and forcing yourself to concentrate on a task.

Although looking busy is highly valued in our culture, taking pauses can actually increase productivity rather than decrease it. Remember that the goal here is not to persevere despite distractions. This is about using the finest techniques to maintain your mental health throughout time.

Here are some suggestions for making the most of your downtime.

Speak With a Friend or Coworker

People provide us with social and emotional cues. It would be good if you have at least one person with a calming presence at your workplace or home. Go speak with them. You don't have to discuss your job; you can talk about your cat, a movie that made you cry, your favorite car brand, or anything else. Quick, informal social connection is a crucial component of mental wellness.

Help Another Person Find a Solution

It often helps you approach your own challenges with fresh perspectives when you assist others in finding solutions to their problems. Additionally, assuming the role of expert or aid will enable you to recognize your worth and improve your self-esteem. For example, you could offer to assist a coworker with a challenging email or offer to help with collecting the trash, or perhaps bring someone else a coffee and inquire about their well-being. These little things can have a major impact on your mental health, which in turn can help you stay motivated and focused.

Take a Walk if You Have the Time

Even 10 minutes of walking can increase creativity. A quick excursion can be the ideal technique to find a solution if you're working on a challenging issue that requires a lot of mental effort. While I'm advocating physically stepping away from your computer (and all other screens), taking a break and getting some exercise will help you return to work with a fresh perspective.

Daydream

Right now, you may be saying: "How can you expect me to daydream at work?" Build it into your schedule if you can, even if it's just for a few minutes. It's good news for your brain and productivity since daydreaming can help you focus and concentrate more.

Staying Committed to Positive Thinking

A positive outlook will help you cope with stress and difficult circumstances in a much more effective manner.

For instance, you might not view stress as a physically harmful or dangerous thing, but rather as a means to a greater aim. Other advantages include strengthening your immune system, developing and maintaining more pleasant relationships, and turning dreams into doable goals.

Let's discuss ways you can maintain a positive mindset.

Music That Soothes Your Mood

Your mood can be improved by music. Many people use songs they love as a way to lift their mood. Some people find that sad music is "beautiful," as it makes them feel better. Some music can bring back memories, provide a distraction from stressful circumstances, and convey powerful messages.

When enjoyed as art, the proper music can be gratifying and uplifting. Therefore, listening to the right music throughout or after a long, difficult workday could possibly improve your mood. So, go ahead—play some Adele, Queen, or Alanis and watch your bad mood vanish.

Have Something to Be Excited About After Work

Even though you might be exhausted after a long day, having plans for after work can make the day seem a bit more promising. A fun-filled evening with your loved ones, colleagues, or friends can help the day fly by.

You don't necessarily have to go out for dinner or drinks as part of your plans. Even making plans for a Netflix marathon might make your work more enjoyable. It's important to design your days so they involve more than just "work." You can discover a good method to balance your personal and professional lives by scheduling some leisure time several days a week.

Run Away From Gossip

Many people live for spreading rumors. But even if something is true, saying it behind someone's back when you wouldn't say it in front of them is wrong. Gossip creates an unsteady, risky, and unpleasant atmosphere at work. Because if you're distributing false information about your coworkers, they're likely doing the same to you.

Even though avoiding gossip can be tricky, resist the urge to participate. If someone tries to share a shocking story about a colleague, politely decline and say you'd prefer not to take part. Although it may seem strange, you'll actually notice that you feel lighter when you're not dragging around secrets. Additionally, you might feel more assured that others are keeping their mouths shut about you when you aren't talking about them. And that's a cause for optimism.

Choose to Start Your Mornings Strong

If you put a positive attitude into practice as soon as you get up in the morning, it will be easier to keep it all day. The dreaded alarm ringing is often an annoyance, which leads to a bad attitude for the rest of the day. Instead, consider some strategies to improve your morning, especially if you're not a morning person. Think about rising an hour or more earlier than normal. This necessitates an earlier bedtime as well!

Give yourself time to indulge in the activities you enjoy but may not always find the time for, such as jogging, taking a hot shower, sipping coffee, and truly preparing breakfast (granola bars and frozen waffles do not qualify). Start your morning doing something you love while savoring a home-cooked meal.

Put on your preferred music or television show. You could even grab a book.

You'll undoubtedly arrive at work in a better mood when your morning is more productive and less hurried. Your day will be infused with that early radiance, and the cycle can repeat itself.

The Best Medicine

Yes, laughter is the best medicine. Laughing has fantastic immediate effects on your body and mindset. Endorphin levels can be elevated, stress can be reduced, and tension can be released.

Laughter and the positive ideas that go along with it have the potential to release neuropeptides that combat stress and other major ailments in the long run. It can also make you happier and assist you in overcoming challenges. By telling more jokes, you can find humor in potentially unpleasant situations while also preparing your body and mind for a more optimistic approach.

Selfless Self-Care

Taking care of your physical and emotional wellness is always important. It can feel overwhelming when you have a full-time job that demands constant interaction with people in high-stress circumstances, whether they are consumers, potential clients, colleagues, or supervisors. Maybe you're in charge of a special task, which can add even more pressure.

Take a step back and reward yourself with something special in order to keep moving forward with an optimistic mentality. Even though it sounds great, self-care doesn't always entail an enchanting nighttime bath with candles and a bottle of wine. Although, if that's your thing, then go for it!

Think about how you can relax, decompress, and spend some "you" time. A face mask, a movie, baking, reading, contacting a friend, ordering takeout, or even just saying "no" to plans and staying in are a few possibilities. You should develop a habit of practicing something every day, no matter what it is. You can assure a more positive attitude when you're working long hours by allowing yourself these breaks. Feeling positive and optimistic will inspire feeling motivated.

Building Momentum and Overcoming Plateaus

What is a plateau? Yes, it's a flat piece of land, but in our case, it refers to a stagnant state where growth no longer takes place. Sometimes, people or situations fall back into a previous state after hitting a plateau. Let's look at some examples.

- You begin your path toward weight loss. You start off dropping weight quickly and then stop. You eventually become discouraged and resume gaining weight.

- You put everything into winning over your partner, but after the relationship peaks, it plateaus.

From commerce to love, from science to war, many things grow until a plateau is reached and then begin to decline, which equalizes the rate of growth.

To overcome these plateaus and build momentum, consider doing the following:

- Get rid of the extra baggage to get ready for the following phase, whether it's guilt, anger, or shame.

- Maintain strong morals and values.

- You have access to resources. Read and learn how to overcome specific challenges, even if it requires you to learn a new skill.

- Document your experiences and what you have learned. This can empower another person who faces similar circumstances.

- Concentrate on increasing value and getting more from your current level.

- Change the smooth road to one with more irregularities and ups and downs. Friction will add more energy for the subsequent growth stage, providing more momentum.

- Determine the issues at your current level and address them.

- Increase leverage from the present stage. Leverage is something you trust. Building this leverage takes time since trust is the hardest and most expensive kind of social currency. People are willing to associate more values with you after you have their trust.

- Slow down and allow a deliberate hump, so that you'll have additional energy as momentum pushes you forward when you accelerate again.

- Use the plateau to observe and appreciate your surroundings. When you're in a speeding car, you seldom have time to focus on the beauty around you. Your only focus is on the road and moving forward. So, appreciate the scenery for a bit once you hit a plateau.

- Accept your current situation and be thankful for being given the opportunity to get where you are.

Everyday Habits to Stay Positive and Focused

In this section, we'll look at several positive behaviors that can change your outlook from being primarily negative to being nearly exclusively positive. Instead of attempting to incorporate all the behaviors at once, pick one and practice it first before adding the next. Try several combinations until you discover one that works best for you.

Keep Ideals From Causing Problems

When changing their attitudes, people often fall into the trap of believing they must always be perfect and perform tasks flawlessly. They become confined and can't be optimistic. It's possible to gradually adopt a positive outlook. Even if you stumble, keep going in this direction and your positive outlook will grow stronger.

However, if you create an impossible standard for yourself and believe you must transform from a pessimist to an optimist at all times, you can find it challenging to live up to that. You can consequently feel like a failure. You become enraged at yourself.

Also, you might give up trying to break this behavior and revert to negative thinking altogether.

Therefore, focus on gradual transformation instead. Try to increase your level of optimism to 60% of the time if it is currently only 40%. When you are comfortable with the new norm, boost it to 80%. If you can, then go up to 100%.

Instead of attempting to meet an unattainable ideal based on perfection, this emphasis on incremental growth is much more realistic and likely to be successful in the long run. You'll also place your focus on what is important instead of trying to chase perfectionism.

Positivity—A Good Way to Start the Day

Your morning routine sets the tone for the rest of the day. You'll find that your day can often be less stressful after a stress-free morning.

How then can you begin your day on a positive note?

Try a three-step combo or something similar that will work for you. For instance, over breakfast, ask yourself what you are grateful for. Then, still very early in the morning, read something uplifting online or in a book. Finally, go for a run or do some other form of exercise. This can help you focus and provide you with enough energy for the rest of the day.

Make Your Environment a Happy Place

Your mood and the way you think about things will be greatly impacted by the information you allow to enter your mind and the company you keep.

Therefore, it's best to decide to:

Accept Information That Is Beneficial to You: Spend less time on media that undermines your self-worth and more time reading inspiring books, seeing uplifting movies, listening to inspirational music, and listening to podcasts and audiobooks produced by positive people.

Increase Your Time Spent With Those That Elevate You: Spend less time—or none at all—with people who just serve to depress you by being negative and criticizing all the time. Being with positive and inspiring people will boost your self-esteem and help you become more positive and focused.

Choose to Be Less Anxious

Anyone's mind can become dominated by the damaging and strong habit of worrying. It might be one of your largest obstacles to optimism, staying focused, and moving forward.

You can reduce your fears by taking these two practical steps:

- Ask yourself: How many of your worries have actually come true? You'll probably discover that the answer is "not many." The majority of the things you worry about throughout your life won't come true. They are merely monsters in your imagination. This question can assist you in conducting a reality check, calming down, and realizing that you have probably simply been creating another fictitious nightmare.

- Focus on solutions and the action you can take. The worries grow stronger in a foggy mind and an inactive body. So, use your question to gain perspective on reality and move out of your worries and into resolution.

Take Care of Your Physical Self

Thinking differently is only one aspect of being an optimist. It also involves taking care of our physical selves. You'll discover that regular exercise, getting enough sleep each night, and eating healthily have a significant impact on your thinking and focus.

If you manage those most simple things improperly, negative thoughts will appear much more often, and you may grow progressively pessimistic and shut down about the possibilities in your life.

Therefore, pay attention to these principles. Simply taking good care of your bodily needs could prevent many troubles in your life.

Ask the Right Questions

This is probably the easiest habit to develop, but it's also one that might be the most essential to cultivating optimism. When we find ourselves in unfavorable, challenging, or unclear circumstances, the questions we ask ourselves daily can make all the difference in the world.

A pessimist will likely ask the following:

- "Why did this happen to me?"

- "Why do bad things always happen to me?"

But an optimist asks questions that allow the mind to be opened to fresh perspectives and opportunities. Here are a few excellent questions to ask to uncover a positive viewpoint:

- "What is at least one positive aspect of this circumstance?"

- "What can I take away from this experience?"

- "What simple action can I take right now to begin resolving this issue?"

This will help you to clear your mind, feel more positive, and sharpen your focus to deal with the situation at hand.

Focus On Finding Solutions

Sitting around and doing nothing about an issue is a surefire way to feel worse about it. Instead, ask questions like the ones in the previous point and be open to the possibilities of the circumstance.

If you are having problems creating an action plan, ask:

- "What is one doable action I can take right now to start things off?"

Then, move on by taking this small step. This simple effort, though, can have a significant impact on your attitude, thinking, and focus. If the step seems overwhelming or simply causes you to put it off, ask the following: "What is a smaller and easier step I can take right now to move forward?"

Sometimes, attempting large strides is far less effective than taking baby steps. If you feel stuck, it's better to move forward slowly until you get out of the rut than not move at all.

More on Gratefulness

We have discussed gratefulness in Chapters 1 and 6, but it is highly relevant to feeling positive and being focused, as it is a very quick and easy approach to increasing the positive energy in your life.

You can achieve this by asking one or more of the following questions:

- "What in my current life can I be grateful for?"

- "Who are three persons in my life for whom I am grateful, and why?"

- "What are three aspects of myself for which I am grateful?"

Answering one or more of these questions during your day will only take a few minutes, but the rewards are priceless.

Never Ever Give Up

You have probably heard the adage, "It's always darkest before dawn." This is a simple but profound and timeless thought that can give you comfort and motivation to keep going when things seem hopeless. When your social abilities and dating life are just poor, it can help you cling on and keep moving forward. When it seems as though business will never pick up, it can be helpful to keep going. Even when things appear dreary, it can still be helpful to put one foot in front of the other.

You might find this adage to be accurate. Something good can always happen, even when things in your business, love life, or general life seem to be at their worst. That's probably because changing your behavior may be imposed upon you when you're in a bad place.

However, it's also possible that life tends to balance itself out when you choose to progress. Something positive always transpires when action is taken as opposed to inaction.

Watching this adage come to pass can help you to believe more strongly that you should retain a positive outlook, take action, and persevere even when things are difficult.

It may take some time to reach a point of effective positivity, motivation, and focus, but as long as you keep going, nothing can stop you. Don't fret if it takes longer than you want. Practice patience and be kind to yourself, and remember—you *will* get there! Allow positivity and focus to run hand-in-hand with self-discipline.

In the next chapter, we'll discuss sustaining a life of self-discipline, measuring your progress, learning from mistakes, and how you can develop habits to sustain self-discipline.

Chapter 8: Sustaining Self-Discipline for a Lifetime of Success

The road to success and achievement is paved with obstacles and troubles. You must act with determination and perseverance in order to overcome them, which of course calls for self-discipline. The acquisition of this skill promotes self-worth and confidence, which in turn promotes happiness and fulfillment.

Self-discipline has various advantages:

- It will give you the drive to get right out of bed in the morning, regardless of how cold it is.

- It will enable you to go on working on a project long after your original enthusiasm has subsided.

- You'll be able to choose things wisely and healthily.

- It will help prevent rash and impulsive behavior.

- You'll be able to break the habit of binge-watching television.

- It will motivate you to work out, such as by taking a stroll or visiting the gym.

- It will provide you the tools you need to beat laziness and procrastination.

- It will serve as a reminder to keep the commitments and decisions you have made to others as well as to yourself.

- You'll be inspired to maintain your diet plan and to withstand the urge to eat unhealthy foods.

- Your capacity to focus when reading, working, or studying will improve.

- It will be crucial in helping you break bad habits.

- You will boldly perform your responsibilities and pursue your objectives diligently.

Achieving even a little portion of this list is a fantastic accomplishment that can improve your life.

You'll find it easier to develop self-discipline if you:

- recognize its significance in your life.

- become conscious of your impulsive behavior and its effects. You will become more certain that you need to improve your life as this awareness grows.

- put forth the effort to carry out your decisions.

- do this despite any feelings of lethargy or the urge to discontinue what you are doing.

Let's explore ways in which you can ensure a lifetime of sustained self-discipline and success.

Staying Accountable and Measuring Progress

There are multiple systems for ensuring accountability. As you create a plan that will meet your needs, take note of the following techniques:

Use an Accountability App

Numerous computer and mobile applications exist that can help you maintain accountability. Some can track your health throughout the day, while others keep track of your goals, time-management skills, and spending patterns in simple to use formats. An accountability tool can help you organize your goal-setting process and develop an organizational structure that is most effective for you.

Obtain Input From Reliable Contacts or Coworkers

Ask a person you trust for their opinion on how you behave yourself at work, your strengths, and your weaknesses. You can find new areas to enhance in the future with the aid of an outside perspective. Additionally, it helps you maintain your accountability to others. If you work on a project with a coworker, for instance, you can ask them for unofficial feedback on how your performance has affected theirs.

Complete a Task Before Beginning Another

Prior to tackling another task, try to focus all of your time and attention on the one you just started. This tactic can help you understand a task better, which will shed light on how long it might take to finish. For instance, if you want to learn a new software program, make a plan to keep your attention solely on the software until you have read the instruction and direction manual. You will then be able to gauge the program's degree of difficulty and how long it might take you to install, use, and become accustomed to it.

Determine Your Values

Think about your core principles and what drives you toward success. With a better understanding of why you choose a specific long-term goal, you may feel more motivated to work toward it and adopt new accountability techniques. To specify a particular element of your value system that you wish to pay particular attention to, write one or two memorable, actionable phrases. You may want to change the statement in the future to better serve another goal. It can be general or more precise.

You can use the following value statements as examples:

- work hard in all situations every day.

- continue to be kind and loving.

- Whenever possible, save money.

Get Ready for a Productive Day

Plan ahead for anything that you might need throughout the day to complete your immediate objectives and any other obligations. It can take less time and effort to start a task when they are prepared, which can motivate you to do it. You may, for instance, open pertinent documents on a digital device or arrange particular objects in your workstation the night before a work meeting. Instead of searching for supplies and setting up your workspace when you go back to work for the meeting, you can use that time to organize your thoughts.

Find Another Person to Hold Accountable

Establish mutual accountability goals and days you wish to check in with each other by meeting with a coworker, business contact, or friend. Finding someone who shares your long-term goal will enable you to provide each other with specialized input. Additionally, you can provide accountability techniques and serve as a source of inspiration throughout the week. If you and a coworker are both writers, for instance, you can decide on a weekly word count target and meet or speak to go over your progress.

Monitor Your Progress

Review your work performance and behavior each month, while acting as your own supervisor. You can create a special plan that meets your needs or model your procedure after that of a supervisor. Check to see whether your expectations are being met and if your goals are achieved in the time frame you have specified. You may use a notebook to keep track of your progress or to compile statistics that are pertinent to your long-term aim, depending on your preferences and skill set.

When evaluating your accountability, take into consideration the following:

- What's your short-term objective for this week, and how are you going about achieving it?

- What is a long-term target that you have?

- What significant metrics have you met this month?

- How long do you spend on each activity or task?

Create a Vision Board

A vision board is a poster featuring images and quotes that inspire you to achieve your goals. Having a visual representation of your long-term or short-term objectives can help you stay motivated on your chosen course. If you already have an interest in creative expression, this tactic might be extremely beneficial. Apply magazine clippings, internet resources, or personal images to any sizable piece of poster board or paper to make your own vision board.

Use a Reward System

Create a reward system for achieving both short-term and long-term goals to encourage yourself to succeed. The size of the prize can be matched to the kind of goal. You might choose to treat yourself to a favorite snack or television show in exchange for achieving the short-term objective of sending three business-related emails every day. For a long-term goal, you can consider booking a trip to celebrate your success and refuel your motivation for future accountability initiatives.

Celebrating Successes and Learning from Mistakes

The road to success can be tough and demanding. It is imperative that you never undermine your own importance throughout this journey! What you do and how you feel matters, perhaps more than you realize. Some people look up to you. There are some who find you inspiring, even when you don't always feel like a shining beacon of hope.

Besides, you need to remain focused and motivated, right?

Therefore, you should always celebrate your successes. Remember how we talked about breaking large goals into smaller objectives? Every small objective you successfully reach is a great victory, and should be celebrated as such! Don't wait for the "big win"—celebrate now.

Why? Because every success that is celebrated reminds you of your skills. It reminds you that all your hard work paid off. Your achievements, however small, deserve to be celebrated, and so do you. Besides, you decided to break free from your "wishing well," leave the forest, and start working tirelessly to reach your goals.

Also, remember that there is victory in both success and failure. You may be thinking: "Is he nuts? Can this be true?" Let me assure you—it *is* true.

Many people make the grave error of making mistakes and becoming disheartened as a result. They regret their failures. They give up because of this and stop trying to discipline themselves.

The truth is, losing is also winning. Failure is a sign of effort. So, it's a win right from the start. Fortunately, it also implies that you gained knowledge; you now understand why what you tried didn't work. You can try something different next time. Get a workout buddy, try it at a different time, unplug your Wi-Fi router—do whatever to increase accountability.

Your failure has taught you something new. You've gained knowledge, which aids in your development.

To have success is to win, but to lose is also to gain. Whatever your outcome, you can view it as a chance to develop, advance, and become better. Give up striving to be perfect at this and instead, simply keep trying.

The next time you fail at something, instead of being disheartened by it, consider it a win. Continue anyway because giving up will simply make your situation worse, which is something you don't want or need right now.

Everyday Habits to Sustaining Self-Discipline

Self-discipline is like a superpower; as you gain it, you might start working out, eating better, meditating, writing, and doing other things more frequently. You might be able to give up smoking and run marathons, establish a blog and write books, read more, get to work earlier, get rid of clutter, and change your financial situation. Even though you are far from flawless, it's okay. You still have much to learn.

However, failing to cultivate self-discipline leads to a host of issues, including clutter, stuff piling up and overpowering you, health issues, distraction, procrastination, financial issues, and more.

The majority of people don't know where to begin or how to maintain self-discipline, which makes it such a crucial ability to master. This section is meant to assist you to achieve this.

Finding the Motivation to Begin

How can you even get motivated to start? Most of us don't want to consider our lack of discipline, much less take several steps to change it.

Realizing that what you are doing isn't working may serve as your motivation. Ignoring the issues just exacerbates the situation. When you make an effort to be disciplined but don't put your all into it, you merely make yourself feel awful. Being completely undisciplined can hurt a lot.

You might form a sincere intention to stop hurting yourself once you recognize that you're doing it. "Alright, enough with making my life worse," you might say. "Let's attempt to mitigate the damage."

In light of this, you can assure yourself that you will:

- start implementing tiny changes to improve the situation.

- act in ways that cause you less pain.

- slightly push yourself into discomfort to strengthen self-discipline over time.

- gain proficiency in self-discipline with some practice.

As you practice, and you feel the need to stop practicing due to mistakes made, keep the above thoughts in mind.

Being Mindful of Urges

You'll have the urge to put off or delay starting something difficult. You are not well served by those urges.

Instead, practice mindfulness around those inclinations and recognize that you are not required to act on them.

Setting up a time during which you can do nothing but one thing is an ideal way to achieve this. For instance, use the next hour to work on writing a chapter for your book. Once you've chosen to write, you'll be able to tell when you have the urge to put off writing or become distracted. When the impulse strikes, remind yourself that you must use the time to write a chapter for your book. You don't allow yourself to do anything else.

It works because you schedule a time during which you carry out only that one particular duty and are able to see your urges flee.

Use this to realize that you don't have to give in to your urges and to become more aware of them.

It's the Small Things

Taking tiny steps is one of the most essential things you can do to improve your self-discipline. The thought of taking on huge, unnerving tasks might be overwhelming. Instead, focus on simple tasks and demands that are too modest to refuse.

Having tax season? Spend five minutes doing it. Do you want to run? Just go for a 10-minute jog. Do you need to work on a report? Just complete the opening sentences. Do you want to organize your space? Pick just five items to purge.

If you concentrate on minor tasks and divide larger undertakings into smaller tasks, you'll be able to improve your self-discipline.

Discomfort Training

We avoid challenging and unpleasant tasks, which is one of the reasons we lack self-discipline. We prefer to carry out simple, convenient tasks. Therefore, we seek distractions rather than dealing with our challenging, uncomfortable projects or finances. Our lives are being ruined by this flight from discomfort.

Declare that you have finished running. You're going to gradually push yourself into discomfort so that you can master it. This is another one of your superpowers if you want it. You're still fine, even when others run away.

Push yourself to your limits one small task at a time, while you analyze your feelings, noticing that your discomfort is not the end of the world. Recognize your incredible qualities and realize that the rewards are well worth the discomfort.

Do Unto Others

When you are facing hardship, consider your deeper motivation: You are not just doing your work, exercise, or meditation for yourself, but also for others.

For instance:

- "I exercise so that I may be healthy—not just for myself, but also to set a good example for my children and other people."

- "I meditate not only to maintain my personal serenity and sanity but also to enable others to do the same."

- "This book is for my kids and anyone else who might find it useful."

- To motivate others, you could write, play music, paint, or draw.

In each case, there is a chance that you may gain something, but you are also helping others. And doing something for the benefit of others is much more inspiring than doing it for your own advantage.

Try it—try helping someone else with a challenging endeavor. In advance, let them know you'll do it with them, and then keep them in mind as you go about it. Check to see if you have more motivation.

Interval Training

You can train yourself using interval training if you put the aforementioned things together into a system of bursts or intervals:

- Decide that you will develop self-discipline and stop hurting yourself.

- Decide on a task to concentrate on, such as writing, sketching, lifting weights, or meditation.

- Set a 10-minute timer. If 10 minutes is too much, five is also acceptable. When you are proficient with 10 minutes, increase to 12 and then 15 minutes. Even when you're kicking it, you usually won't need to go for longer than 15 to 20 minutes.

- Simply observe your urges as they come and go, or act on your discomfort by doing the activity.

- You should allow yourself a five-minute pause once the timer rings.

- Repeat.

You can exercise for short periods or perhaps for an hour or two. After that, take a longer break before performing another round of intervals. This type of interval training is efficient since it isn't too difficult—you can accomplish a lot by training yourself in discomfort while suppressing urges of procrastination or distraction.

You're Not in This Alone

You don't need to do this alone. You can get support from your friends, family, and online acquaintances. By contacting those in your vicinity and requesting their assistance, you can put together a support group.

Many people choose to skip this because they feel ashamed of their lack of self-discipline. They believe their actions are unacceptable. That is untrue. Actually, we all behave in this manner; we're just reluctant to reveal it to one another. The reality is that people will love you more, trust you more, and relate to you more if you reveal your "dark" side to them. So, don't be reluctant to establish a vulnerable connection with others.

Show some courage and seek assistance. Then allow yourself to be supported while you work to push yourself into discomfort, develop self-discipline, pursue motivation, work persistently toward your final goal, and hurt yourself less.

You have all this power. It is time to use it.

Conclusion

Nothing worthwhile in life is possible without self-discipline. In our own life, the "magic well" may appear in a variety of ways, such as get-rich-quick schemes, or an addiction to television, video games, or parties.

All of these things, like in Larry, Ben, and Charlie's story, provide momentary pleasure. Nonetheless, they are fleeting and ephemeral. Get rid of all magic wells in your life and commit to exercising self-discipline if you want to succeed in life.

In Chapter 1, we had an overview of self-discipline. We saw that with a lack of self-discipline, we can suffer low self-esteem, experience laziness, and procrastinate often. We'll easily give in to temptations, feel generally negative, fear failure, and have no goal or purpose in life. When we lack ambition, willpower, and motivation, we don't have the foundation on which to build self-discipline.

Having the self-control to avoid unhealthy excess of something that can have negative repercussions is what it means to be disciplined. Its ability to put off short-term pleasure and instant gratification in favor of longer-term benefits or more rewarding results is one of its distinguishing characteristics, even when doing so involves effort and patience. The term typically generates some discomfort and resistance due to the mistaken idea that it is unpleasant and requires too much work and sacrifice.

In Chapter 2, we discussed willpower—how it works and is connected to self-discipline and self-control. According to the strength model, all people have a limited amount of willpower that can be exhausted. However, the process model suggests that willpower is subjective and can change according to a person's needs. That which is viewed as critical at one moment can seem less critical in the next.

Willpower has a quality of self-control. It is best described as a strong resolve that helps one to complete a difficult endeavor. It helps you accomplish several goals you have in mind. Examples include reducing spending, improving one's health, or quitting smoking. To accomplish long-term goals, a person must be able to restrain negative thinking, mood, or urge as well as the ability to put off enjoyment and resist temptations in the short term. It also requires deliberate, conscious self-regulation.

In Chapter 3, we talked about the nature of procrastination, its dangers, and how to remain focused and productive. We saw that procrastination is the act of delaying or postponing a task or set of duties. It is the force that keeps you from finishing the tasks that you started. Our brains are wired to seek quick rewards, also called instant gratification. We don't want to focus on long-term rewards, as these rewards are still out of reach.

However, we can overcome procrastination by instating deadlines, breaking larger goals into smaller objectives, prioritizing, using to-do lists, resisting the urge for perfectionism, linking our work to our goals, and efficiently managing our time. We can succeed by staying calm, making a habit of working diligently, and focusing on greater productivity. Once you have determined the cause of wanting to procrastinate, you can address the issue and overcome it.

In Chapter 4, we explored the importance of setting realistic and attainable goals. We saw that setting a realistic goal encourages us to move forward, boosts our morale, is a way to measure progress, helps us prioritize, and makes us accountable. We'll find it easier to move toward the end goal by setting milestones. As we are all unique and have our own circumstances, skills, and motivations, we should never compare our goals to those of others.

Long-term goals can be broken into short-term objectives by doing something like in this example:

- This week, gather suggestions and comments from the customer service representatives.

- This month, assess the current procedure and pinpoint areas that need to be improved.

- In two months, gather client feedback and identify recurring issues.

- Within three months, submit a business case explaining your suggested changes to executive stakeholders.

- In four months, complete your project plan.

- In five months, train the customer service staff in the new procedures.

- In six months, implement the new process across all customer service teams.

In Chapter 5, we covered time management and how to go about prioritizing tasks. We learned that the ability of time management to give people a purpose for their time and allow them to make the most of it is what makes it valuable. In the corporate sector, it is used to set goals and expectations for businesses and the employees who work there. Employees who manage their time well can generate high-quality work and meet their goals. Managers can set achievable objectives and recognize employee potential with the help of time management.

Tasks can be prioritized by first determining which tasks are the most important. Then, work on these tasks can be scheduled. It is important to stick to this schedule at all times. Next, set boundaries by reducing distractions. Each task should be prioritized individually. If possible, less important tasks can be delegated to reliable colleagues. Don't shy away from technology—use it to manage your time more efficiently.

In Chapter 6, we talked about developing resilience. We saw that resilience is the capacity to successfully deal with challenging or difficult life conditions. Flexibility in one's thinking, feeling, and behavior is necessary for being able to respond to both internal and external challenges. It's crucial to keep in mind that you must gradually build your skill set to become resilient. You have to work hard to build resilience, and there will probably be challenges along the road.

The 7 Cs model of resilience explains it as follows:

Coping: We need to create stress-relieving coping skills.

Character: To feel deserving, to make moral choices, and to contribute to society.

Competence: This is the ability to discern how to successfully handle a situation.

Confidence: People increase their self-confidence by exhibiting their talent in common situations.

Control: People can solve issues by having a solid understanding of internal control rather than by being passive recipients of events.

Contribution: A great motivator is having a sense of purpose. Reciprocal relationships are strengthened by giving back to the community.

Connection: Close ties to family, friends, and the community offer a sense of safety and belonging.

In Chapter 7, we discussed how to stay focused and motivated. You can achieve this by first determining what motivates you. We further focused on using time blocks to work on tasks that are important to you. Take a break when things begin to feel overwhelming.

To stay focused, you can listen to uplifting music, plan something exciting after work, refrain from gossip, fill yourself with more humor, and take good care of yourself. If you have reached a plateau and growth no longer seems possible, use this time to appreciate your surroundings, regain inner strength, and build enough momentum to propel yourself toward success once again.

In Chapter 8, we covered how you can sustain self-discipline and ensure a lifetime of success. To stay accountable and monitor your progress, you can use an accountability app on either your computer or smartphone. You can also ask trusted colleagues or friends for input and improve on their suggested areas. Also, aim to be more successful by defining your values and being ready to be productive every single day.

Always celebrate your victories; whether you've achieved a short-term objective or a long-term goal. This will remind you that your hard work matters and that you are making a difference. Never give up! Just keep pushing forward. Find your motivation, be mindful of urges that threaten to distract you, and allow your goals to benefit not only yourself but other people too. If anything, always remember that you are not alone!

The great thing about this book is that it is a tool you can use over and over again. Whenever you feel stuck, lost, or unproductive, just look at the suggested habits once again. Rekindle the fire and passionately work toward your goal. Success is within reach!

If you found this book to be inspirational, helpful, or life-changing (hopefully all of these!), kindly leave a positive review so I am enabled to reach more people. The world needs us! Let's step up and help those who need it!

Luke Thybulle

FREE E-Book:
Discover How to Finally Conquer Your Fears

PLUS I'll share with you
<u>My #1 Secret To Guaranteed Success...</u>
See firsthand how I direct my focus to live a life full of energy, passion and confidence.

- Luke Thybulle

<u>www.northstarreaders.com/luke-thybulle/conquer-your-fears</u>

References

Amaresan, S. (2021, June 9). *10 creative ways to keep a positive attitude no matter what.* Hubspot. https://blog.hubspot.com/service/positive-attitude

Babauta, L. (2017, May 23). *A guide to developing the self-discipline habit.* Zen Habits. https://zenhabits.net/self-discipline/

Baratta, K. (2023, January 24). *How to prioritize goals in work and life.* Prialto. https://www.prialto.com/blog/how-to-prioritize-goals

Baumeister, R. F., & Tierney, J. (2011). *Willpower: Rediscovering the greatest human strength.* The Penguin Press.

Baumeister, R. F., Vohs, K. D., & Tice, D. M. (2007). The strength model of self-control. *Current Directions in Psychological Science, 16*(6), 351–355. https://doi.org/10.1111/j.1467-8721.2007.00534.x

Burka, J. B., & Yuen, L. M. (2008). *Procrastination: Why you do it, what to do about it now.* Da Capo Press.

Campbell, R. (2022, November 5). *7 time management tips for students.* Top Universities. https://www.topuniversities.com/blog/7-time-management-tips-students

Caunt, J. (2010). *Organise yourself: Clear the clutter, take charge of your time, manage information* (3rd ed.). Kogan Page.

Cherry, K. (2009, January 28). *10 ways to build resilience.* Verywell Mind. https://www.verywellmind.com/ways-to-become-more-resilient-2795063

Cherry, K. (2021, April 28). *What is willpower?* Verywell Mind. https://www.verywellmind.com/willpower-101-the-psychology-of-self-control-2795041

Clarke, J. (2021, October 7). *Healthy ways to celebrate success.* Verywell Mind. https://www.verywellmind.com/healthy-ways-to-celebrate-success-4163887

Clear, J. (2015, June 11). *Procrastination: A scientific guide on how to stop procrastinating.* James Clear. https://jamesclear.com/procrastination#:~:text=Here

Das, R. (2022, November 21). *11 fascinating plateau strategies for uplifting your plateaued stagnant life and career.* LyfasOne. https://lyfas.com/mental-health/11-fascinating-plateau-strategies-for-uplifting-your-stagnant-life-and-career/rupam_lyfas/

Davis, J. (2020, March 27). *Overcoming setbacks: How to thrive in the face of adversity.* LinkedIn. https://www.linkedin.com/pulse/overcoming-setbacks-how-thrive-face-adversity-james-davis

Di Maio, S., Keller, J., Job, V., Felsenberg, D., Ertel, W., Schwarzer, R., & Knoll, N. (2020). Health demands moderate the link between willpower beliefs and physical activity in patients with knee osteoarthritis. *International Journal of Behavioral Medicine, 27*(4), 406–414. https://doi.org/10.1007/s12529-020-09865-w

Dienstmann, G. (2021). *Mindful self-discipline: Living with purpose and achieving your goals in a world of distractions.* LiveAndDare Publications.

Digitalsunilsah. (2021, November 2). *A story of self discipline which will change your life.* Spiritual Success. https://www.spiritualsuccess.in/2021/11/story-of-self-discipline.html

Doerr, J. (2018). *Measure what matters: How Google, Bono, and the Gates Foundation rock the world with OKRs.* Portfolio/Penguin.

Edberg, H. (2013, October 24). *9 simple habits to stay positive in life.* Personal Excellence. https://personalexcellence.co/blog/positivity/

Ellis, K. (1998). *The magic lamp: Goal setting for people who hate setting goals.* Three Rivers Press.

Fiore, N. A. (2010). *The now habit at work: Perform optimally, maintain focus, and ignite motivation in yourself and others.* John Wiley & Sons.

Francis, Z., Sieber, V., & Job, V. (2019). You seem tired, but so am I: Willpower theories and intention to provide support in romantic relationships. *Journal of*

Social and Personal Relationships, *37*(3). https://doi.org/10.1177/0265407519877238

Gleeson, B. (2020, August 25). *9 powerful ways to cultivate extreme self-discipline.* Forbes. https://www.forbes.com/sites/brentgleeson/2020/08/25/8-powerful-ways-to-cultivate-extreme-self-discipline/?sh=5daf8576182d

Greitens, E. (2015). *Resilience: Hard-won wisdom for living a better life.* Houghton Mifflin Harcourt.

Halvorson, C. (2015, October 12). *11 habits of people who always reach their goals.* Insider. https://www.businessinsider.com/11-habits-of-people-who-always-reach-their-goals-2015-10

Hasa. (2022, November 21). *What is the difference between willpower and discipline.* Pediaa. https://pediaa.com/what-is-the-difference-between-willpower-and-discipline/

Heath, R. (2009). *Celebrating failure: The power of taking risks, making mistakes, and thinking big.* Career Press.

How to set realistic goals: The ultimate guide to achieve them. (2022, November 25). Timeular. https://timeular.com/blog/how-set-realistic-goals/

Hurley, K. (2022, July 14). *What is resilience? Your guide to facing life's challenges, adversities, and crises.* Everyday Health. https://www.everydayhealth.com/wellness/resilience/

Indeed Editorial Team. (2023a, February 24). *Holding yourself accountable: Definition and strategies.* Indeed Career Guide. https://www.indeed.com/career-advice/career-development/holding-yourself-accountable

Indeed Editorial Team. (2023b, February 27). *Mental focus: 10 ways to improve your concentration.* Indeed Career Guide. https://www.indeed.com/career-advice/career-development/ways-to-improve-focus

Indeed Editorial Team. (2023c, March 11). *How to prioritize workplace tasks (with 5 steps and tips).* Indeed Career Guide. https://www.indeed.com/career-advice/career-development/prioritize-tasks-in-the-workplace

Inzlicht, M., Schmeichel, B. J., & Macrae, C. N. (2014). Why self-control seems (but may not be) limited. *Trends in Cognitive Sciences, 18*(3), 127–133. https://doi.org/10.1016/j.tics.2013.12.009

Keenan, M. (2022, June 8). *21 effective time management tips for managing your workload.* Shopify. https://www.shopify.com/za/blog/120436229-time-management-tips

Kennedy, T. (2008, March 12). *How to build self discipline to excel in life.* Lifehack. https://www.lifehack.org/articles/productivity/self-discipline-the-foundation-of-productive-living.html

King, S. (2018). *Overcoming plateaus to achieve sustainable business growth.* Growthforce.

https://www.growthforce.com/blog/overcoming-plateaus-to-achieve-sustainable-business-growth

Konze, A.-K., Rivkin, W., & Schmidt, K.-H. (2018). Can faith move mountains? How implicit theories about willpower moderate the adverse effect of daily emotional dissonance on ego-depletion at work and its spillover to the home-domain. *European Journal of Work and Organizational Psychology, 28*(2), 137–149. https://doi.org/10.1080/1359432x.2018.1560269

Kruse, K. (2015). *15 secrets successful people know about time management: The productivity habits of 7 billionaires, 13 Olympic athletes, 29 straight-A students, and 239 entrepreneurs.* The Kruse Group.

Leone, C. (2016). *Self-discipline: Why self-discipline is lacking in most and how to unleash it now.* Createspace Independent Publishing Platform.

Lieberman, C. (2019, March 25). *Why you procrastinate (it has nothing to do with self-control).* The New York Times. https://www.nytimes.com/2019/03/25/smarter-living/why-you-procrastinate-it-has-nothing-to-do-with-self-control.html

Loyd, A. (2015). *Beyond willpower: The secret principle to achieving success in life, love, and happiness.* Harmony.

MacNeil, C. (2022, October 27). *How to accomplish big things with long-term goals.* Asana. https://asana.com/resources/long-term-goals

Martins, J. (2021, July 7). *The secret to stop procrastinating at work.* Asana. https://asana.com/resources/tips-stop-procrastinating

Mayo Clinic Staff. (2022, July 14). *Resilience: Build skills to endure hardship.* Mayo Clinic. https://www.mayoclinic.org/tests-procedures/resilience-training/in-depth/resilience/art-20046311#

Meadows, M. (2017). *The ultimate focus strategy: How to set the right goals, develop powerful focus, stick to the process, and achieve success.* Meadows Publishing.

Mind Tools Content Team. (2023). *Self-Discipline: Persisting until you reach your goals.* Mindtools. https://www.mindtools.com/adjf7nz/self-discipline

Moltz, B. (2022, July 19). *How to increase your focus and not get distracted.* American Express. https://www.americanexpress.com/en-us/business/trends-and-insights/articles/increase-your-focus-reduce-distractions-tips/

Morin, A. (2017, July 17). *5 ways to turn your mistake into A valuable life lesson.* Forbes. https://www.forbes.com/sites/amymorin/2017/07/17/5-ways-to-turn-your-mistake-into-a-valuable-life-lesson/?sh=2d3e6cf21c01

Motivation: How to get started and staying motivated. (2022, July). Health Direct.

https://www.healthdirect.gov.au/motivation-how-to-get-started-and-staying-motivated

Mueller, S. (2022, December 7). *How to stay motivated – stay focused & positive.* Values Inspired Advocacy. https://viadvocacy.com/Articles/how-to-stay-motivated-stay-focused-positive

Murnan, A. (2022, August 22). *Willpower: What it is and how to improve it.* MedicalNewsToday. https://www.medicalnewstoday.com/articles/will power#effects

Nantham, S. (2021, February 2). *12 simple ways to stay focused and increase productivity.* Profit.co. https://www.profit.co/blog/task-management/12-simple-ways-to-stay-focused-and-increase-productivity/

Newport, C. (2016). *Deep work: Rules for focused success in a distracted world.* Grand Central Publishing.

Niven, P. R., & Lamorte, B. (2016). *Objectives and key results: Driving focus, alignment, and engagement with OKRs.* John Wiley & Sons.

Oaten, M., & Cheng, K. (2006). Longitudinal gains in self-regulation from regular physical exercise. *British Journal of Health Psychology, 11*(4), 717–733. https://doi.org/10.1348/135910706x96481

Oman, D., Shapiro, S. L., Thoresen, C. E., Plante, T. G., & Flinders, T. (2008). Meditation lowers stress and supports forgiveness among college students: A randomized controlled trial. *Journal of American*

College Health, *56*(5), 569–578. https://doi.org/10.3200/jach.56.5.569-578

Prater, M. (2018, July 6). *Secrets of self-discipline: How to be disciplined in 15 imperfect steps.* Hubspot. https://blog.hubspot.com/sales/self-discipline

Purposefairy.com. (2022, September 10). *7 great ways to stop procrastinating and motivate yourself to study.* The Epoch Times. https://www.theepochtimes.com/7-great-ways-to-stop-procrastinating-and-motivate-yourself-to-study_4722678.html?utm_medium=GoogleAds&utm_source=PerfmaxM&utm_campaign=PM_max_brand_L2non41228&gclid=CjwKCAjwrdmhBhBBEiwA4Hx5gzLNr7ghiWwCP8O1rsUu6osMjEW51LiiJWC1N_AYSooQiB6PaVukPhoCUs4QAvD_BwE

Robertson, C. (2015, March 12). *10 daily habits that will give you incredible willpower.* Willpowered. http://willpowered.com/learn/daily-willpower-habits

Robson, D. (2023, January 3). *The mindset that brings unlimited willpower.* BBC. https://www.bbc.com/worklife/article/20230103-how-to-strengthen-willpower

Ross. (2020, March 31). *Why self-discipline is important (11 key reasons).* The Disciplined Rebel. https://disciplinedrebel.com/ultimate-guide-to-developing-self-discipline-part-1-why-is-self-discipline-important/#Why_Self-Discipline_Can_Be_Challenging

RSA. (2012). *Willpower: Self-control, decision fatigue, and energy.* In YouTube. https://www.youtube.com/watch?v=vefDeoXCBbk

Ryan, F. (2014). *Willpower for dummies.* John Wiley & Sons, Ltd.

Salgado, H. (2021, April 7). *9 great habits for mental resilience.* LinkedIn. https://www.linkedin.com/pulse/9-great-habits-mental-resilience-hec-salgado

Salzgeber, N. (2018). *Stop procrastinating: A simple guide to hacking laziness, building self-discipline, and overcoming procrastination.* CreateSpace Independent Publishing Platform.

Sandberg, S., & Grant, A. (2017). *Option B: Facing adversity, building resilience, and finding joy.* Ebury Publishing.

Sasson, R. (2010, March 5). *Lack of self-discipline—what are the reasons.* Success Consciousness. https://www.successconsciousness.com/blog/inner-strength/lack-of-self-discipline/

Sasson, R. (2020a, April 1). *Self-discipline benefits and its importance in your life.* Success Consciousness. https://www.successconsciousness.com/blog/inner-strength/self-discipline/

Sasson, R. (2020b, June 10). *What is self-discipline—definitions and meaning.* Success Consciousness. https://www.successconsciousness.com/blog/inner-strength/what-is-self-discipline/

Scott, C. (2018, September 21). *3 types of self-discipline you need to accomplish your vision.* Carjie Scott Ed.D. https://carjiescott.com/2018/09/21/3-types-of-self-discipline-you-need-to-accomplish-your-vision/

Selhub, E. (2019). *The stress management handbook: A practical guide to staying calm, keeping cool, and avoiding blow-ups.* Skyhorse Publishing.

Soong, J. (2011, November 29). *The secret (and surprising) power of naps.* WebMD. https://www.webmd.com/balance/features/the-secret-and-surprising-power-of-naps

Stark, A. (2019, July 11). *How to discipline yourself with 10 habits.* Medium. https://medium.com/@akostark/how-to-discipline-yourself-with-10-habits-c46ad7304319

Syed, M. (2015). *Black box thinking: Why most people never learn from their mistakes—but some do.* Portfolio/Penguin.

The Oracles. (2018, December 7). *"Most people probably would have stopped"—8 tips on overcoming even the most crippling setbacks.* CNBC Make It. https://www.cnbc.com/2018/12/07/8-tips-on-overcoming-even-the-most-crippling-setbacks.html

Timely Team. (2023, March 29). *How to set realistic goals.* Timely. https://timelyapp.com/blog/how-to-set-realistic-goals

Tomiyama, A. (2019). Self-control and academic achievement. *Annual Review of Psychology.* https://doi.org/10.1146/annurev-psych-010418-

Tracy, B. (2007). *Eat that frog! 21 great ways to stop procrastinating and get more done in less time.* Berrett-Koehler Publishers.

Tracy, B. (2010). *No excuses! The power of self-discipline.* Vanguard Press.

Tracy, B. (2019, September 6). *Goal setting—your guide to setting and achieving goals.* Brian Tracy. https://www.briantracy.com/blog/personal-success/goal-setting/

Tsuei, J. (2021, September 14). *12 tips for getting (and staying) motivated at work.* Clockwise. https://www.getclockwise.com/blog/get-motivated-focus-at-work

Vranich, B. (2010). *Get a grip: Your two-week mental makeover.* John Wiley & Sons.

Walsh, R. (2008). *Time management: Proven techniques for making every minute count.* Adams Business.

Warnock, B. (2014, May 30). *10 reasons why setting goals is important when it comes to success online.* Blue Host Blog. https://www.bluehost.com/blog/10-reasons-setting-goals-important-comes-success-online/

Waters, S. (2022, October 12). *Eliminate distractions at work for your most productive day yet.* BetterUp.

https://www.betterup.com/blog/how-to-avoid-distractions

Weliver, D. (2023, March 22). *Manage yourself: 10 ways to make yourself accountable at work, in life, and with money.* Money under 30. https://www.moneyunder30.com/manage-yourself-10-ways-to-make-yourself-accountable-at-work-in-life-and-with-money

Wellbeing. (2023, April 11). *10 ways to boost your personal resilience and better cope with stress.* Zurich. https://www.zurich.com/en/media/magazine/2021/10-steps-that-will-increase-your-personal-resilience

Wesley, B. (2017). *The power of adversity: The setbacks of life are only setups for extraordinary comebacks.* Power of Adversity.

Wigmore, I., & Lutkevich, B. (2023, February). *Time management.* WhatIs.com. https://www.techtarget.com/whatis/definition/time-management

Wilson, S. B., & Dobson, M. S. (2008). *Goal setting: How to create an action plan and achieve your goals.* American Management Association.

Wise, N. (2018). *The self-discipline handbook: Simple ways to cultivate self-discipline, build confidence, and obtain your goals.* Skyhorse Publishing.